ONCE UPON A FAIRY TALE

I0804522

ONCE UPON A FAIRY TALE
Volume II

Favorite Folk and Fairy Tales
by the
Brothers Grimm

Translated and Interpreted by
Norbert Glas, M.D.

RUDOLF STEINER COLLEGE PRESS

First published as individual pamphlets by Norbert Glas, M.D., by whom all rights are reserved: *Snow-White Put Right*, 1944; *The Handless Maiden*, 1944; *Snow-White and Rose-Red*, 1945; *Cinderella*, 1946; *Red Riding Hood*, 1947; *Mary's Child*, 1949; *Sleeping Beauty* (*Briar Rose*), 1950.

First complete edition Copyright 1976 by St. George Publications. Published by St. George Publications by arrangement with Norbert Glas, M.D.

Cover Art © 1995 by Barbara Klocek

© 1995 Rudolf Steiner College Press
Revised and Edited Edition
ISBN 0-916786-04-8

LIBRARY OF CONGRESS CATALOG CARD NUMBER 76-15100

All rights reserved.
No part of this book may be copied in any form whatsoever without the written consent of the publisher.

Foreword to the Second Edition

The worldwide popularity of Walt Disney's film *Snow White and the Seven Dwarfs* compelled me to write about the real meaning of fairy tales. That film destroys for both children and adults the spiritual content of a beautiful tale. With a deep understanding for their content, the Brothers Grimm collected [European] fairy tales over a period of many years. Reading these original stories carefully, one discovers that each phrase, even each word, is deliberately chosen to stress the true background of the events told.

In our times it is increasingly necessary to give young children fantasy images brought from a higher world. The soul of the unspoiled child is not interested in the intellectual tales and anecdotes it is so often fed nowadays. The children become spiritually starved and dry in their thinking.

The examples given in these seven fairy tales may arouse devotion for the greatness of their content. Parents and teachers may become inspired to tell the stories to the children. It has to be added, perhaps, that we have to offer the stories as they are, without speaking to the children, of course, about their meaning.

I am grateful to the publishers for reprinting what was written many years ago, for world conditions have not improved since then and, at present, even more courage is needed than before to struggle against the failings in our age.

Norbert Glas, M.D.
Gloucester, England
March, 1976

Table of Contents

Volume II

Little Red Cap

INTRODUCTION

ALMOST all great poetry depicts the development of the human soul and the struggle and pain involved therein. The human being conquers or is overcome; his own powers bring him forward or else his weakness destroys him. In his struggles he may also receive help in manifold ways. The visible and the invisible worlds work with him or against him. The way in which we tread our path through fortune and misfortune makes up the drama of life. The meaning of all poetry is after all to reveal this drama in story and picture in order that we may better understand our own existence.

The stories collected by the Brothers Grimm offer an almost limitless supply of images representing such events taking place within the human soul. In modern times, as a result of childhood spent in towns and of the mechanization of life, it is more and more difficult to apprehend the intimate stirrings of the soul and the spirit, and yet of course the real development of the human being takes place through inner changes and not through outer ones. As a result of modern conditions it may be difficult for many people to discover the hidden meaning in fairy tales. This, however, is only so for the adult. The child who is in the happy position of being able to listen to the fairy story —inasmuch as it is not distorted by alterations—lives so fully in the content of the pictures that any explanation is unnecessary and would be quite a mistake. The grown-up, however, should bear in full consciousness the content offered the child through the story, knowing that it is not a fantastic or beautiful and poetic lie, but a truthful imagination of the path of human evolution.

Little Red Cap

(Red Riding Hood)

ONCE upon a time there lived a sweet little maiden, who was very much beloved by every one who saw her. But her grandmother loved her so much that she could never give her enough. Once she presented her with a little cap of red velvet and it fitted her so well that she would never wear anything else, so she was called Little Red Cap. One day her mother said to her: "Come, Little Red Cap, here is a piece of cake, and a bottle of wine. Take these to your grandmother; she is ill and weak and they will refresh her. Go, before it gets too hot, and while you are on your way behave modestly and do not run off the path lest you should fall and break the glass, and then your grandmother will have nothing. When you go into her room, do not forget to say 'Good morning,' and do not look about in all the corners."

"Everything will be all right," said Little Red Cap, taking her mother's hand.

The grandmother dwelt far off in the forest, half an hour's walk from the village. As Little Red Cap entered the forest she met the wolf. She did not know what an evil beast he was and so she was not at all afraid of him. "Good day, Little Red Cap," said he.

"Many thanks, wolf."

"Whither away so early, Red Cap?"

"To my grandmother's."

"What are you carrying under your apron?"

"Cake and wine. Yesterday we baked and Grandmother, who is weak and ill, will enjoy this and gain strength."

"Red Cap, where does your grandmother live?"

"A good quarter of an hour's walk further on in the forest. The cottage stands under three great oak trees; beneath them are some nutbushes, which you know, of course," said Little Red Cap. But the wolf thought to himself: "She is a nice tender thing, a fat morsel, and will taste much better than the old woman. I must act craftily that I may snap them both up."

He walked a little while by her side and then he said: "Little Red Cap, look at the beautiful flowers which grow around you. Why do you not look about you? I believe you don't hear how beautifully the little birds sing? You walk on as if you were going to school and it is so merry out here in the forest."

Little Red Cap opened her eyes, and when she saw how the sunbeams danced to and fro through the trees and how everywhere there grew beautiful flowers, she thought: "If I take grandmother a fresh nosegay, that will be a joy for her, too. It is so early in the day that I shall nevertheless arrive on time."

She ran off the path into the wood and looked for flowers. When she had picked one, she thought that more beautiful ones might grow further on and kept going deeper and deeper into the forest. The wolf, however, walked straight to the house of the grandmother and knocked at the door.

"Who's there?"

"Little Red Cap, bringing you some cake and wine. Open the door."

"Press on the latch," cried the grandmother, "I am too weak and cannot get up."

The wolf pressed on the latch and the door flew open; he went without a word straight to the bed of the grandmother and swallowed her up. Then he dressed in her clothes, put on her cap, got into her bed and drew the curtain.

All this time Little Red Cap was still gathering flowers, and when she had plucked so many that she could not carry another one, she remembered her grandmother and set out on the way to her. When she arrived, she wondered that the door was open. And when she entered the room and everything seemed to be so strange in it, she thought: "Oh goodness! How afraid I begin to feel today. I have always liked to visit grandmother at other times."

"Good morning," she called, but received no answer. So she went up to the bed, and drew back the curtain. There lay the grandmother. She had drawn her cap far down over her face and looked so peculiar. "Ah, grandmother," she said, "what great ears you have !"

"All the better to hear you with!"

"Ah, grandmother, what great eyes you have!"

"All the better to see you with!"

"Ah, grandmother, what great hands you have!"

"All the better to seize you with!"

"But, grandmother, what a horrible great snout you have!"

"All the better to devour you with!" And scarcely had the wolf said this than he sprang out of bed and swallowed up poor Little Red Cap. As soon as the wolf had satisfied his greedy desire he lay down again in the bed, went to sleep and began to snore very loudly.

The huntsman, passing by, thought: "How loudly the old woman snores! I must see if there is anything the matter." So he entered the room and when he came to the bed he saw the wolf lying in it. "What! Do I find you here, you old sinner?" he said. "I have been looking for you for a long time."

Then he took aim with his gun, but it occurred to him that the wolf might have eaten the grandmother and that she might be saved, so he did not shoot. Instead, he took some scissors and began to cut open the belly of the sleeping wolf. When he had made the first few cuts he saw a little red cap shining. He cut a little further, and the maiden leaped out.

"Oh, how frightened I was!" she exclaimed. "How dark it was in the wolf's body!"

Then the old grandmother also came out alive, but she could scarcely breathe. Little Red Cap, however, quickly fetched some big stones, and with these they filled the body of the wolf. When he woke up he wanted to spring away; but the stones were so heavy that he sank to the ground immediately and fell down dead.

Now all three of them were very happy. The huntsman skinned the wolf, took his fur and went home with it.

The grandmother ate the cake and drank the wine little Red Cap had brought her and recovered again.

Little Red Cap said to herself: "Never again in my life will I stray alone from the path and run into the forest, when my mother has forbidden it."

Little Red Cap

COMMENTARY

ONCE upon a time there lived a sweet little maiden, who was very much beloved by every one who saw her. But her grandmother loved her so much that she could never give her enough.

"Little Red Cap" begins by telling of the strong tie the child has with her grandmother. This points to the great influence of heredity upon the human being. In these opening words the fairy tale has imprinted upon it the stamp of something patriarchal, even of an Old Testament quality, and it persists throughout the whole story: the human being owes what he is to his ancestors.

Once she presented her with a little cap of red velvet and it fitted her so well that she would never wear anything else, so she was called Little Red Cap.

This shows clearly the influence of the grandmother. The child receives from her a covering, a sheath, which endows her with particular characteristics. The being of the young girl is thus determined by her ancestor. The red color clearly points to the red blood and the forces of heredity which are carried by the blood. With little Red Cap this influence is so strong that it takes hold and imprints itself upon her whole being. In olden times the head covering worn by a human being was of definite significance, expressing the class or status to which the individual belonged. From the headdress of a woman, it could often be seen whether she was married or not. The degree of seniority reached by a man in his calling could be recognized by what he wore on his head. In many religious organizations something of this is still to be found. Think, for example, of the cardinal's hat. Another example is the "mortarboard" of a university graduate—a sign set upon his head to denote a particular rank. Relics of such customs can be seen in the cap of a railway engineer or of a postman and so on. Even if for some reason there is no longer a complete uniform, the person will at least be given a cap to put on the head! Moreover, in olden times most callings were inherited, and so also was the corresponding sign. The force of heredity is so strong in Red Cap, influencing her so powerfully, that the blood forces work even up into her head, and this is indicated by her red cap. Not only has Red Cap inherited through her grandmother the gifts from her ancestors in special abundance, but to her grandmother also she owes her name. Right at the beginning we are told of something characteristic of the child indicating, though in a very delicate way, a quality with an inherent danger—the little cap is so pretty and fits so well that the child does not want to wear anything else. Here, there is a touch of pride, and the little girl will no doubt have to undergo certain trials and experiences. She is proud of something towards which she herself has contributed nothing. The fairy tale points to a time when inherited gifts will no longer suffice for human life. It will be far more important then what the individual himself does and achieves.

One day her mother said to her: "Come, Little Red Cap, here is a piece of cake, and a bottle of wine. Take these to your grandmother; she is ill and weak and they will refresh her. Go, before it gets too hot, and while you are on your way behave modestly and do not run off the path lest you should fall and break the glass, and then your grandmother will have nothing. When you go into her room, do not forget to say 'Good morning,' and do not look about in all the corners."

Now the mother appears, and she plays a very significant part. She tries to create a balance between the old, outworn forces embodied in the grandmother and the youthful, as yet unexpressed forces in Red Cap, which bear the seed of the future. The mother knows that the grandmother needs help. Her time is past. The power of heredity is fading. The old woman is weak and ill and in need of assistance. She can only be sustained by something powerful enough to enable her to pass over into another period of time. She must be able to leave the old patriarchal time in which life is determined by the blood, and to enter a new time in which the power of blood relationship is more and more overcome and the way is opened to the individuality. It is important to understand that this change from the old to the new is the very essence of Christianity. This is not meant dogmatically, but from a world-historical, world-evolutionary point of view. It is the individual human being to whom Christ shows a path. More and more will depend on the individual's own ego. In order to reach our goal we must undergo many trials and tests and must learn to develop our own powers.

Little Red Cap is sent on her errand to overcome the old forces of heredity. The mother, who watches over the whole process like a sheltering spirit, gives the child those forces which alone can prevail in this moment of development: bread and wine, the symbols of the Christian sacrament. It can have no other meaning than this when in the fairy tale the mother gives bread and wine to heal the grandmother. In the Christian church the Christ comes to the human being in the bread and wine; through them the sickness inherited through the blood is healed. In reality, it is a holy communion to which Red Cap is sent by her mother. The mother knows of the dangers to which the soul is exposed when it sets out on such a path leading into the future. This mother, however, also intends that the grandmother should be healed, and trusts that her impressive warning will suffice to keep the child on the right path.

Red Cap, who has received her name from her ancestor and who is also proud of her beautiful little cap, listens willingly to her mother. Innocently she promises:

> "Everything will be all right," said Little Red Cap, taking her mother's hand.

We get the impression that before this the child lived entirely under the protection of her mother and that this protection was even strengthened by the presence of the old grandmother, now lying ill. From the moment when Red Cap is left to herself, however, everything changes.

> The grandmother dwelt far off in the forest, half an hour's walk from the village. As Little Red Cap entered the forest she met the wolf.

It lies in the nature of almost any trial undergone by a human being that he is alone in it. He may receive help in the end, but in the first place he must be alone, thrown back upon himself. In a fairy tale the forest, into which a being goes or is led, is almost without exception a picture for the soul awakening to inner perception and then having to enter various realms. Hansel and Gretel are sent into the forest; Snow White goes into the forest; the poor man in "The Two Brothers" goes into the forest and sees the bird with the gold feathers. In Daeumerling's wanderings the little tailor goes into "a great forest," the miller in "The Handless Maiden" went into the forest to fetch wood—and many other instances could be cited. Again and again when a human being is to meet a being from the supersensible realm, the picture of the forest appears in the fairy tale. The forest indicates the realm just beyond the limits of the material world. In it the soul enters the realm of life. Even as in ordinary life, walking beneath the overhanging branches of a forest, treading upon the soft moss, surrounded by delicate rustlings and sounds, we may feel near to the elementary forces of growth, so the human being may have the picture of the forest inwardly before him as he enters a realm of the supersensible world. Dante, describing in the *Divine Comedy* the soul's path as it takes its course through the spiritual world, begins with the words:

> In the middle of the journey of our life I (came to) myself in a dark wood (where) the straight way was lost.

When, however, the human being does reach this world—comes into the "forest"—he is then exposed to great dangers. These are the trials through which he has to go on the path of his development. The hindering powers come to meet him; they may appear in animal forms before the soul. Often there are three, perhaps very fearful, animal-like monsters. The *Edda* tells of Fenris-wolf, Hel, and a terrible snake, Ioerrnungandr. Dante describes a leopard, a lion and a she-wolf. In these great epics are depicted the three main forces which desire to seize the human soul and destroy it. The wolf usually represents the covetous, grasping, insatiable being which drives the human being through life in blood-thirsty greed. In Dante the she-wolf is "torn by every passion . . . and a she-wolf that looked full of all cravings in her leanness; and has ere now made many live in sorrow."

It is this animal which Red Cap meets; the others do not come into the picture. The child is quite unprepared for such a meeting and in her innocence does not even recognize the wickedness of the beast.

She did not know what an evil beast he was and so she was not at all afraid of him. "Good day, Little Red Cap," said he.

"Many thanks, wolf."

"Whither away so early, Red Cap?"

"To my grandmother's."

"What are you carrying under your apron?"

"Cake and wine. Yesterday we baked and Grandmother, who is weak and ill, will enjoy this and gain strength."

"Red Cap, where does your grandmother live?"

"A good quarter of an hour's walk further on in the forest. The cottage stands under three great oak trees; beneath them are some nutbushes, which you know, of course," said Little Red Cap.

If we meet the adversary we should recognise him at once in order to fight him successfully. Dante, for example, recognises the enemy appearing before him in the form of the three beasts and therefore finds a leader in Virgil, who can guide him safely through all dangers. Red Cap is at first not so fortunate. She trusts the wolf, which at once shows its superiority; it knows the child's particular weakness and makes use of it.

The wolf, as we have said, is in this tale the symbol of greed, of insatiable desire. Once the human being has fallen a prey to these forces, he is subject to them in all actions. In the course of development, the human being strives to draw his will impulses from the forces of his own true individuality and not merely from the sphere of instincts. This aspect of human development comes to expression in manifold ways in the cultural life as a whole. Often it seems that long periods of time are needed to accomplish any step in the development of consciousness towards which humanity is striving.

The signs of our struggle against the animal instincts can be seen in the taming of wild animals—animals in whom the human being sees pictured those forces of evil which rise up within him, and against which he has to fight to retain his humanity. Probably there is some connection between the great variety of dogs, the fact that different people are often especially fond of particular breeds, and the way in which an individual may experience a feeling of joy in that one or other aspect of the "wolf" has been overcome. This feeling often remains unconscious in the human being, and yet he may be drawn just to that animal which represents for him what he himself has achieved—or would hope to achieve! It can often be a source of great satisfaction to experience the devotion of a dog to the person of its owner. It can be like a call to further attainment!

Moreover, it is interesting to remember that dogs also take on characteristics in some way reminiscent of their owner. There then arises that interesting interplay between the dog and its master. On the other hand, some people have a great dislike of dogs, and it seems then that perhaps the original wolf nature appears too much on the surface and they do not wish to see it.

In the wolf of the fairy tale, all the evil qualities symbolized by this animal come to expression.

> But the wolf thought to himself: "She is a nice tender thing, a fat morsel, and will taste much better than the old woman. I must act craftily that I may snap them both up."

It is important to realize that the wicked animal wants to destroy them both—the old dying forces embodied in the grandmother and the forces, as yet weak but belonging to the future, which appear in Red Cap.

And now there takes place a scene in which the child is led into temptation.

> He walked a little while by her side and then he said: "Little Red Cap, look at the beautiful flowers which grow around you. Why do you not look about you? I believe you don't hear how beautifully the little birds sing? You walk on as if you were going to school and it is so merry out here in the forest."

The mother had given the little girl certain directions for her own protection. The tempter, in the guise of the wolf, works slyly and systematically to gain power over the child. In the "forest," the first realm of the supersensible world, we are exposed to all kinds of temptation. Red Cap is now led by the wolf himself. Here there is no Virgil who comes at once to help, as it was with Dante. The wicked animal attacks where he thinks to reach his aim most quickly. He turns the child's attention to the beauty of the world. This is an easy way to win over Little Red Cap. She had not been able to resist the pretty little cap her grandmother gave her and had become quite proud. Then the wolf laughs at her for keeping so exactly to her mother's directions and for walking so correctly along the path, as though she were going to school. In this way he hints at the possibility of behaving according to her own freedom, without so great a sense of duty.

> Little Red Cap opened her eyes, and when she saw how the sunbeams danced to and fro through the trees, and how everywhere

there grew beautiful flowers, she thought: "If I take grandmother a fresh nosegay that will be a joy for her too. It is so early in the day that I shall nevertheless arrive in time." When she had picked one, she thought that more beautiful ones might grow further on and kept going deeper and deeper into the forest.

Quickly she falls into the clutches of the wolf. Simply to mention the beauty of the world was enough to make her open her eyes. With Red Cap it was just as it so often is in the act of succumbing to a temptation; the human soul gives way to illusions concerning its own good intentions. Little Red Cap really wants to enjoy the freedom and beauty herself, but she persuades herself that it would be good to bring something beautiful to her grandmother. And just because of her unclear feeling—is she looking at all the beauty for herself or is she only doing it in order to give joy to her grandmother?—she really does stray from the right path.

The wolf, however, walked straight to the house of the grandmother and knocked at the door.

From the moment Little Red Cap leaves the right path, about which her mother had warned, she delivers her grandmother and herself into the power of the tempter. And what does the tempter want? On the one hand he wants to prevent the old forces of the grandmother from being rejuvenated through the healing forces of Christianity, through the bread and the wine. On the other hand he wants to destroy the childlike impulses of the future embodied in Red Cap. In his unspeakable greed he wants to have everything. He goes to work very slyly, planting, however, just through his great cleverness and logic, the seed of death in his own destiny.

"Who's there?"

"Little Red Cap, bringing you some cake and wine. Open the door."

"Press on the latch," cried the Grandmother, "I am too ill and cannot get up."

The wolf pressed on the latch and the door flew open; he went without a word straight to the bed of the grandmother and swallowed her up. Then he dressed in her clothes, put on her cap, got into her bed and drew the curtain.

The wolf soon has done with the old woman. She is already so weak and tottering that she cannot even tell who is coming to her—whether it is Red Cap bringing her the healing forces of youth, or the devil who wants to destroy her. Without any opposition, she simply lets the adversary come in.

All this time Little Red Cap was still gathering flowers and when she had plucked so many that she could not carry another one, she remembered her grandmother and set out on her way to her.

The child is so greedy for the treasures of the world of beauty, the flowers, that she picks as many blossoms as possible until she can carry no more. And here we notice that her intention to bring the grandmother a bunch was after all only to deceive herself. While picking the flowers, she had quite forgotten the old grandmother. Only when she has picked so many that she can carry no more does Red Cap recall that she is on the way to her grandmother's house, and starts off again at last.

She wondered that the door was open. And when she entered the room and everything seemed so strange in it, she thought: "Oh, goodness, how afraid I begin to feel today. I have always liked to visit grandmother at other times."

Now for the first time Red Cap is afraid. Before, when she first met the wolf, there was no fear in her. Only now, after she has fallen into temptation, has trusted the wolf, told him about her grandmother and then, following his hint, has taken advantage of her freedom, only now does a dark feeling of guilt arise in her heart. We are reminded of how Adam, after the fall into sin, was suddenly filled with fear when he heard the voice of God. In the fairy tale it is touched upon much more lightly. The little girl remembers that something should have happened since she left home. Filled with a feeling of foreboding, she remembers her mother's original command: "And when you go into her room, do not forget to say 'Good morning,' and do not look about in all the corners." The first thing she does in the anxiety of her bad conscience is to return to the good instructions of her mother.

"Good morning," she called, but received no answer. So she went up to the bed and drew back the curtain. There lay the grandmother. She had drawn her cap far down over her face and looked so peculiar.

Red Cap now behaves very well, and does not look around the room, just as her mother had bade her. Unhappily, after having followed the tempter, this good advice no longer helps her. As a matter of fact, we are led to think that it would have been all the better if Red Cap had given a really good look round the room.

> "Ah, grandmother, what great ears you have!"
> "All the better to hear you with!"
> "Ah, grandmother, what great eyes you have!"
> "All the better to see you with!"
> "Ah, grandmother, what great hands you have!"
> "All the better to seize you with!"

The child feels more and more ill at ease, but is not yet able to see what is the matter. Red Cap does not perceive the source of the evil. She tests herself with the threefold question without having more than a dim intuition of the danger. That the wolf has ears is not so unusual, that he has eyes does not distinguish him so very much from other beings. With the third question Red Cap does come nearer the point at issue, but she is still unclear about the situation because she calls the animal's paws "hands," characteristic of a human being. Then suddenly full consciousness dawns, and we see the terrible fear which accompanies it. That is why the fourth question is worded differently from the others.

> "But grandmother, what a horrible great snout you have!"
> "All the better to devour you with!" And scarcely had the wolf said this, than he sprang out of bed and swallowed up poor Little Red Cap.

Her recognition is described clearly in that she uses the word "snout" instead of "mouth." The child sees that she is face to face with an animal and not with her grandmother. The jaws of a wolf are particularly characteristic of its nature. The whole power of the wolfish instincts are expressed in the snout. With its jaws it overcomes its prey and wounds its opponent. There lies the danger. In her fright—and the imaginative listener experiences this too!—Red Cap is rooted to the ground. She does nothing, is unable to run away and must undergo a great trial. She is engulfed in the body of the wolf—a picture of the great trial undergone by the soul after the meeting with the adversary.

Again and again in myths the wild dragon appears, who lusts after human souls and swallows them. This is another version of the picture of the test through which the hierophant had to go while being initiated into the secrets of the ancient mysteries. This is how, as Rudolf Steiner has shown, the swallowing of Jonah by the whale is to be understood—"And Jonah was in the belly of the fish three days and three nights" (Jonah 2:1). That the sojourn of Jonah in the belly of the whale was of significance can be seen from the fact that Christ says: "For as Jonah was three days and three nights in the whale's belly, so shall the Son of Man be three days and three nights in the heart of the earth" (Matthew 12:40). Red Cap and the grandmother have to go through a dark time of trial before they can be saved. But to be freed from their pain and guilt they need real help, and such help now approaches.

As soon as the wolf had satisfied his greedy desire he lay down again in the bed, went to sleep and began to snore very loudly.

The huntsman, passing by, thought: "How loudly the old woman snores. I must see if there is anything the matter."

The hunter in a fairy tale is always of special significance. Very often it is he who helps the human being out of a difficult situation through knowledge and understanding of the circumstances. In this way he is often a determining factor in the destiny of the beings in the story. In "Snow White" it is the huntsman to whom the wicked queen delivers Snow White to be killed. It is in his hands whether she shall live or die. He understands the true way of destiny and acts accordingly. In other fairy stories it is the huntsman who is the strong person and has the powers necessary for the overcoming of evil. Often he has a certain wisdom of life, a clear thinking, as a result of which he acts very consciously. In this connection it is illuminating to read the story of "The Wise Hunter" by Grimm. When destiny must be set aright and the human individuality is to be led back to the proper path, there appears again and again in the fairy story the picture of the huntsman. In "The Twelve Huntsmen," the king's son, through an inner weakness, does not hold to his true bride. The bride dresses, with other maidens, in the garments of a huntsman and thereby brings about the necessary changes. In a still more wonderful way, the ruling power of the huntsman may be seen in the long and complex story "The Two Brothers." Here we see also how a strong-willed determination can help to bring about the right solution to the crises of destiny.

Different callings have very definite significance in the fairy tale. It can be shown, for instance, that the miller usually appears in the story when it concerns the weight and depression of earthly conditions, such as poverty—mention of this is made in the explanation of "The Handless Maiden." The huntsman, however, in a true fairy tale, points to forces connected with the inpouring of influences from the stars. In olden times there existed a profound knowledge of the relationship between the stars and humanity. The influence of Sagittarius—and it is obvious that the huntsman is a picture for this constellation—can be understood in connection with those forces which the human being brings to bear upon his lower nature, to overcome the animal in himself. This is why the huntsman is superior to this animal nature. Either he overcomes the animals who are wicked, like the wolf in "Little Red Cap" and the dragon in "The Two Brothers," or he ennobles them, making them serve him, as is so beautifully described in the story of "The Two Brothers." The way the huntsman goes to work always has an element of wisdom in it. His wisdom has nothing to do with mere intellectual cleverness in regard to material things, in the way expressed by the tailor in a fairy tale. Sagittarius works in the individual element of human nature. He helps the human being to find the right path of destiny, particularly at times when, as it has happened to Red Cap, this path has been lost.

That is why, in the moment when for Red Cap everything seems to be lost, suddenly the huntsman appears and sets things right.

> So he entered the room and when he came to the bed he saw the wolf lying in it. "What! Do I find you here, you old sinner?" he said. "I've been looking for you for a long time." Then he took aim with his gun, but it occurred to him that the wolf might have eaten the grandmother and that she still might be saved. So he did not shoot. Instead, he took some scissors and began to cut open the belly of the sleeping wolf.

The thoughtful action of the huntsman reveals his clear consciousness; he knows exactly what he must do and why. A fine touch, indicating this, is the fact that he uses scissors to cut open the belly of the wolf. Scissors are always a sign of cleverness in the fairy tale. That is why the tailor always has his scissors. In the story of "The Seven Little Kids" the old goat—whose character resembles that of a tailor—takes a pair of scissors to cut open the stomach of the wolf.

When he had made the first few cuts he saw a little red cap shining. He cut a little further, and the maiden leaped out.

"Oh, how frightened I was!" she exclaimed. "How dark it was in the wolf's body!"

With the huntsman's help, Little Red Cap is freed first. From the way she now behaves and speaks, it is clear that she has learned much through her experience inside the evil animal. The maiden is now quite awake in her being.

Then the old grandmother came out alive, but she could scarcely breathe.

In the story it seems quite natural that Red Cap should jump out of the belly of the wolf, quite fresh and alive. She has all the forces of the future in her. She had only to undergo the great trial, to use the forces of Sagittarius, and then she could find the impetus for a new life. But for the old grandmother it is very different and we have cause to be anxious about her. She was already weak, and now she has had to go through all this misfortune. What will become of her?

Little Red Cap, however, fetched some big stones and with these they filled the body of the wolf. When he woke up he wanted to spring away; but the stones were so heavy that he sank to the ground and fell down dead.

What does Red Cap do first? She has made a great advance in her development and the first thing she thinks of is the final overcoming of the wolf. The wolf had betrayed her into abandoning herself too completely to the forces of the world. He had led her to the darkness and diverted her from fulfilling her duty to her grandmother. Now she completely puts an end to the power of the wolf over her and gives him the stones he deserves. He falls to the ground, back to the dead earth.

Now all three of them were happy. The huntsman skinned the wolf, took his fur and went home with it.

The grandmother ate the cake and drank the wine Little Red Cap had brought her and recovered again.

Little Red Cap said to herself: "Never again in my life will I stray alone from the path and run into the forest, when my mother has forbidden it."

The huntsman, the great helper of the human individuality, can now withdraw, taking with him the skin of the wild animal.

The sick grandmother must be properly healed, and this is only possible in that she is at last able to receive the remedy by which her outworn forces can be rejuvenated. She eats the cake, the bread, and drinks the wine; in other words, she receives the holy communion. Thus she overcomes the sick, failing forces of heredity and is able to make way for the youthful forces of individuality. In this moment there takes place the great change from the ancient patriarchal time of the Old Testament to the new time of Christian development. Red Cap, who already bears within her all the youth and freshness of the future, has learned to tread the path into the future in the proper stages. She will never wander alone in the "forest" again. She will never go without a guide into the supersensible realms if in her own development she is not yet ripe enough.

The fairy tale "Little Red Cap" describes thus in a most wonderful way the victory of the human soul over the forces of temptation, which want to prevent it from treading the true path into the future.

Mary's Child

INTRODUCTION

THERE are moments of particular importance in the development of the human being. At such times a person may be attentive to destiny or he may be blind to it and run the risk of overlooking a task which is awaiting him. Such decisive moments might be called crises, and much will depend on whether a crisis is recognized and properly overcome. Many fairy tales describe in pictures how the human being in his little boat of life approaches the perilous streams of destiny. He must often take long detours to prevent the stream from dashing him against the deadly rocks. In the development of a child the period of puberty is such a time of danger. We will try to show how this period of life, with all its troubles and striving, is described in detail in this fairy tale by the Brothers Grimm.

What is the special significance of puberty? At this time the growing human being is rudely awakened from the dreams of childhood and abandoned to the chaotic experiences of earthly life. But what do we mean by the dreams of childhood?

In the period preceding this critical phase the child was still enveloped by forces brought from the realm beyond the earth—a realm which has been described, perhaps a little theoretically, as the world of innocence. It may also be called the state of Paradise. Every child going through puberty repeats in an individual way what humanity as a whole experienced in the distant past: the temptation by Lucifer and the subsequent fall into material existence. For humanity it will take a long time before the premature entry into the sense world is redeemed. In the life of an individual too, it often takes a long time to come through the crisis of adolescence, which is really the reflection of an ancient event in the history of mankind. This important time of development may be far more easily understood if such facts are borne in mind.

A fairy tale like "Mary's Child" can be a source of great

enlightenment, because it shows the close connection between the destiny of the individual and that of the whole of humanity.

Mary's Child

ON the edge of a great forest there lived a woodcutter with his wife, who had an only child, a girl three years old. But they were so poor that they could no longer earn their daily bread, and did not know what they should give her to eat. One morning the woodcutter went out full of sorrow to his work in the forest, and while he was cutting wood, suddenly there stood before him a beautiful tall woman, who had a crown of shining stars on her head, and who said to him: "I am the Virgin Mary, mother of the little Christ Child. You are poor and needy. Bring your child to me, I will take her with me, and be her mother, and care for her." The woodcutter obeyed, fetched his child, and gave her to the Virgin Mary, who took her with her up to Heaven. Here she fared well; she ate sugar-bread and drank sweet milk; and her clothes were of gold, and the little angels played with her.

Now, when she was fourteen years old, the Virgin Mary called her one day and said: "Dear child, I am about to make a long journey, so take into your keeping the keys of the thirteen doors of the Kingdom of Heaven. Twelve of these you may open, and look at the splendour which is within, but the thirteenth door, to which this little key belongs, is forbidden you. Beware that you open it not, or you will be unhappy."

Mary's Child promised to be obedient, and when the Virgin Mary was gone, she began to view the dwellings of the Kingdom of Heaven. Each day she opened one, until she had made the round of the twelve. In each of them sat one Apostle in the midst of a great radiance, and she rejoiced in all the magnificence and splendour, and the little angels who always accompanied her rejoiced with her. Then the forbidden door alone remained, and she felt a great desire to know what could be hidden behind it, and said to the angels: "I will not open it entirely, and I will not go inside, but I will unlock it, so that we can see just a little through the chink."

"Oh, no," said the little angels, "that would be a sin. The

Virgin Mary has forbidden it, and it might easily cause your unhappiness."

Then she was silent, but the desire in her heart was not stilled, but gnawed there and pecked on it properly and let her have no rest. And once when the angels had all gone out, she thought: "Now I am quite alone, and I could peep in. If I do, no one will know it." She sought out the key, and when she had got it in her hand, she put it also in the lock, and when she had put it in, she turned it round as well. Then the door flew open, and there she saw the Trinity, sitting in fire and radiance. She stayed there awhile and looked at everything in amazement; then she touched the radiance a little with her finger, and her finger became quite golden. Immediately she felt a mighty fear. She banged the door violently and ran away. But do what she might, her anguish would not quit her, and her heart beat continually, and would not become still: the gold, too, stayed on her finger, and would not go away, however much she washed and rubbed it.

It was not long before the Virgin Mary came back from her journey. She called Mary's Child before her, and asked to have the keys of heaven back. When the child gave back the bunch, the Virgin looked into her eyes and said: "You have not opened the thirteenth door, have you?"

"No," she replied.

Then Mother Mary laid her hand on the girl's heart, and felt how it beat and beat, and saw right well that she had disobeyed her orders and had opened the door. Then she said once again: "Have you really not done it?"

"No," said the girl for the second time.

Then she caught sight of the finger that had become golden from touching the heavenly fire, and saw well that the child had sinned, and said for the third time: "Have you not done it?"

"No," said the girl for the third time.

Then said the Virgin Mary: "You have not obeyed me, and besides that you have lied. You are no longer worthy to be in heaven."

Then Mary's Child fell into a deep sleep, and when she awoke she lay on the earth below, in the midst of a wilderness. She wanted to cry out, but she could bring forth no sound. She sprang up and wanted to run away, but whithersoever she turned, she was continually held back by thick hedges of thorns through which she could not break. In the solitude, in which she was enclosed, there stood an old hollow tree, and this had to be her dwellng place. Into this she crept when night came, and here she slept. Here, too, she found a protection from storm and rain. But it was a miserable life, and bitterly did she weep, when she remembered how lovely it had been in heaven, and how the angels had played with her. Roots and wild berries were her only food, and for those she sought as far as she could go. In the autumn she picked up the fallen nuts and leaves, and carried them into the hole. The nuts were her food in winter, and when snow and ice came, she crept among the leaves like a poor little animal, that she might not freeze. Before long her clothes were all torn, and one bit of them after another fell off her. As soon as the sun shone warm again, she went out and sat in front of the tree, and her long hair covered her on all sides like a mantle. Thus she sat year after year, and felt the distress and the misery of the world.

One day, when the trees were once more clothed in fresh green, the King of the country was hunting in the forest, and followed a roe, and as it had fled into the thicket which shut in this part of the forest, he got off his horse, tore the bushes asunder, and cut himself a path with his sword. When he had at last forced his way through, he saw a maiden of wondrous beauty sitting under the tree; she sat there and was entirely covered with her golden hair down to the toes of her feet. He stood still and looked at her full of surprise; then he spoke to her and said: "Who are you? Why are you sitting here in solitude?" But Mary's Child gave no answer, because she could not open her mouth. The King continued: "Will you go with me to my castle?" Then she just nodded her head a little. The King took her in his arms, carried her to his horse, and rode home with her, and when he reached the royal castle he caused her to be dressed in beautiful garments, and gave her all things in abundance. Although she could not speak, she was still so beautiful and charming that he began to love her with all his heart, and it was not long before he married her.

After a year or so had passed, the Queen brought a son into the world. Thereupon the Virgin Mary appeared to her in the night when she lay in her bed alone, and said: "If you will tell the truth and confess that you did unlock the forbidden door, I will open your mouth and give you back your speech, but if you persevere in your sin, and deny obstinately, I will take your newborn child away with me."

Then the Queen was permitted to answer, but she remained stubborn and said: "No, I did not open the forbidden door," and the Virgin Mary took the new-born child from her arms and vanished with it.

Next morning, when the child was not to be found, there was a murmur among the people that the Queen was a man-eater, and had put her own child to death. She heard all this and could say nothing to the contrary, but the King would not believe it, because he loved her so much.

When a year had gone by the Queen again bore a son, and in the night the Virgin Mary again came to her and said: "If you will confess that you opened the forbidden door, I will give you your child back and untie your tongue; but if you continue in sin and deny it, I will take away with me this new child also."

Then the Queen again said: "No, I did not open the forbidden door," and the Virgin Mary took the child out of her arms, and went away with her to heaven. Next morning, when this child also had disappeared, the people declared quite loudly that the Queen had devoured it, and the King's councillors demanded that she should be brought to justice. The King, however, loved her so dearly that he would not believe it and commanded the councillors under pain of death not to say any more about it.

The following year the Queen gave birth to a beautiful little daughter, and for the third time the Virgin Mary appeared to her in the night and said: "Follow me." She took the Queen by the hand and led her to heaven, and showed her there her two eldest children, who smiled at her, and were playing with the ball of the world. When the Queen rejoiced thereat, the Virgin Mary said: "Is your heart not yet softened? If you will own that you opened the forbidden door, I will give you back your two little sons."

But for the third time the Queen answered: "No, I did not open the forbidden door." Then the Virgin Mary let her sink down to earth once more, and took from her likewise her third child.

Next morning, when the matter became publicly known, all the people cried loudly: "The Queen is a man-eater! She must be judged," and the King was no longer able to restrain his councillors. Thereupon a trial was held, and as she could not answer, and defend herself, she was condemned to be burnt at the stake.

As the fire began to burn round about her, the hard ice of pride melted; her heart was moved by repentance, and she thought: "If I could but confess before my death that I opened the door." Then her voice came back to her, and she cried out loudly: "Yes, Mary, I did it!" And straightaway rain fell from heaven and extinguished the flames of fire, and a light broke forth above her, and the Virgin Mary descended with the two little sons by her side, and the new-born daughter in her arms.

She spoke kindly to her and said: "He who repents his sin and acknowledges it is forgiven." Then she gave her the three children, untied her tongue, and granted her happiness for her whole life.

Mary's Child

COMMENTARY

ON the edge of a great forest there lived a woodcutter with his wife, who had an only child, a girl three years old.

At the very beginning of the story an important situation is depicted. The forest is a picture of the world of life with all its secrets. We have described this in connection with other stories, such as "Red Riding Hood" and "Snow-White." When in the fairy tale revelations come to a person from the spiritual world, they may be experienced, for example, in the forest. Sometimes the individual goes into the forest and is translated into another world and meets other beings. The father in "Mary's Child" is a woodcutter, and in fairy tales this is a significant calling. The woodcutter is the one who cuts down the trees of the forest. We know the feeling of regret, even of pain, when many trees are being felled in a beautiful forest. It can be felt as the destruction of a world filled with wonderful secrets and riddles. The woodcutter is the dry practical man who keeps having to destroy the rampant life of the "forest." He is the person who is quite given over to the cares of earth and must work by the sweat of his brow. It is worth noting that one of the most well known and beloved fairy tales, "Hansel and Gretel," begins with almost identical words:

In a great forest, there lived a poor woodcutter with his wife . . .

Another important fact introduced in the first sentences of the story is the age of the child—she is three years old. The third year is a very decisive one, during which a child gradually begins to be able to think, and this results in moments when he is able for the first time to feel himself as an individual being. Rudolf Steiner pointed to the fact that about this time a child often has some decisive experience of himself as an individual. He mentions Jean Paul as an example, who relates how at the age of three he experienced himself as an individual. It is for this reason that memory usually goes back until about the third year. Another good example among many others would be Ludwig Richter, the painter. In his autobiography Richter writes: "One of my earliest memories is a visit to Grandfather Mueller. . . . I was then about three years old." And the delightful story of how he went alone into the town and got lost trying to pick star flowers is to be found in *Lebenserinnerungen eines deutschen Malers.** This experience in the third year is very important, because it marks the beginning of the process whereby as life proceeds we gradually find our own higher selves upon earth. To recognize the ego means no less than to recognize here in the physical world and in one's own body that spiritual being who existed in the spiritual world before birth. The whole of life is really the search of the human soul for the higher self—the ego—and the experience of the third year is like a shining in of the ego, a prophecy of what the future must contain.

It is said of the parents of Mary's Child:

> But they were so poor that they could no longer earn their daily bread, and did not know what they should give her to eat.

This is a picture of great poverty. The first meeting with the earthly world must be terrifying for the child, if even the comforting symbol of the earth body, the bread, is lacking. With the sacramental bread, the Host, the body is purified and healed. In the house of Mary's Child, there is no bread, and with this the fairy tale indicates that human beings have descended deeply into the life of earth and are far from redemption and purification. Similarly, in "Hansel and Gretel" we read: "and once, when a great tax was levied throughout the land, he could no longer buy any bread."

> One morning the woodcutter went out full of sorrow to his work in the forest, and while he was cutting wood, suddenly there stood before him a beautiful tall woman, who had a crown of shining stars on her head, and who said to him: "I am the Virgin Mary, mother of the little Christ Child. You are poor and needy. Bring your child to me. I'll take her with me, and be her mother, and care for her."

The ego lights up in the three year old child for the first time. Having formed the bodily dwelling with the help of powers inherited from father and mother, the individuality feels

* Frankfurt am Main, Verlag von Johannes Alt, 1898.

that the task ahead is to mold and shape this dwelling in order to live within it as fully as possible. If this happens easily the child remains healthy and no dangerous crisis occurs. But if the individual already feels the brittleness of his own little house, a severe crisis may well follow. The frailty of the inherited body is often indicated in the paintings of the birth of the Jesus Child. The physical deterioration is shown by the ruined house in which the birth takes place. There are, for example, three different pictures by Albrecht Altdorfer of the birth of Christ. We see crumbling walls, broken tiles, ceilings with torn rafters. In one painting all that is left of the house are two stone pillars with only a few rotting remains of the wooden beams hanging from them. All is poverty and misery, and we know that only because the spiritual light streams in from above while the angels dance their protecting measures, and because the Holy Mother will nourish the Child, can He remain alive. If even the Jesus Child needs Mary's protecting hand before the Saviour may enter the body, how much more does the little human child need care and protection before it can take possession of the fragile dwelling. So in this fairy tale the Mother of God herself appears and takes the soul into her own care until it has grown capable of independence.

The woodcutter obeyed, fetched his child, and gave her to the Virgin Mary, who took her with her up to heaven. Here she fared well; she ate sugar bread, and drank sweet milk; her clothes were of gold, and the little angels played with her.

The earthly parents are unable to give Mary's Child the necessary food. This happens, alas, only too often! Even if children receive the right physical nourishment, how often do we allow them to starve spiritually. In the first years of life above all the human being needs beauty in his environment, and the loving warmth and understanding of the adults around him. The light and air that penetrate from the spiritual world at this time must not be too frequently cut off by the smoke that rises from the physical world, or the child will not be able to breathe, and will tend to return to the world from which it has descended. The young heroine of the story is cared for by the Heavenly Mother, because the earthly one is not able to do it.

The developing human being must be so guided that in time he will be in a position to lead his own life, and for this the ego must be strengthened. Proper nourishment can be of great value; the Child of Mary received sugar-bread and milk. Rudolf Steiner often says that sugar is a substance which strengthens the ego. It is, of course, well known that certain conditions of fatigue through over-exertion can be relieved by giving sufficient doses of sugar. Muscular fatigue is simply an indication that the individual is no longer capable of controlling his body through the forces of his will.* Milk, on the other hand, helps a person to live in the world in a balanced way, without forgetting his spiritual origin.** How could the Mother Mary nourish the child better than by giving her sugar-bread and milk to prepare her for life upon earth? Sugar strengthens the individuality. Milk opens the soul to the whole universe, and bread heals the weakness of the earthly body. As long as the child remains within the care of Mother Mary, she is clothed in the golden robes of divine wisdom. The angels play with her.

Now when she was fourteen years old, the Virgin Mary called her one day and said: "Dear Child, I am about to make a long journey, so take into your keeping the keys of the thirteen doors of the Kingdom of Heaven. Twelve of these you may open, and look at the splendor which is within, but the thirteenth door, to which this little key belongs, is forbidden you. Beware that you open it not or you will be unhappy."

Until the fourteenth year, it is possible for a child to grow up entirely under the wings of divine beings, but there always comes a time when the soul must of its own accord enter the earthly world. Before this change takes place, everyone goes through a kind of trial which is like a repetition of the ancient trial of humanity. In the story, the sustaining Mother of God now withdraws, and Mary's Child must learn to see for herself what lies behind the doors of Heaven. She is allowed to open twelve doors, but she must not unlock the thirteenth. Why? Clearly because she is not mature enough.

Mary's Child promised to be obedient, and when the Virgin Mary was gone, she began to view the dwellings of the Kingdom of Heaven. Each day she opened one, until she had made the round of the twelve.

* "In the consuming of sugar a kind of innocent egoism is brought about."

** "The forces which come to the human being through nourishment from milk prepare him to take his place as a human creature upon earth, and bring him into contact with earthly conditions without really chaining him there. They make him into a citizen of the whole solar system at the same place."
—Rudolf Steiner, The Hague, March 13, 1921.

In each of them sat one Apostle in the midst of a great radiance, and she rejoiced in all the magnificence and splendor, and the little angels who always accompanied her rejoiced with her.

We must ask ourselves: what is it that the human soul has to experience up to the time of puberty? The soul comes from the heavenly world where it has learned how the human body must be formed upon Earth out of the forces of the stars. In old paintings we often see how the Zodiac is brought into connection with the human form. In the constellation of Taurus were recognized the forces which formed the larynx, or in the constellation of Leo the forces of the heart, in Pisces of the feet, and so on. According to its destiny, before its descent the soul received within itself all the knowledge and forces necessary to build up the body later on. At birth the little child received from father and mother the fragile dwelling of the body. As Rudolf Steiner has described it, this first body serves only as a model for the soul to use in building the dwelling which will really be its own. The soul does this through the wisdom it has received from the great Zodiac. By the time of puberty this work should have been completed. The twelve dwellings of the human body are then ready for the soul to enter, each formed in the wisdom of one of the twelve zodiacal forces. Mary's Child, now having attained her fourteenth year, may open all twelve doors with her keys. She sees behind each door a representative of one of the constellations of the Zodiac, namely one of the twelve disciples. As the Sun is surrounded by the twelve zodiacal constellations, so is Christ surrounded by the twelve apostles.

Then the forbidden door alone remained, and she felt a great desire to know what could be hidden behind it, and said to the angels: "I will not open it entirely, and I will not go inside, but I will unlock it so that we can see just a little through the chink."

"Oh, no," said the little angels, "that would be a sin. The Virgin Mary has forbidden it and it might easily cause your unhappiness."

It is a great danger for the soul that it is tempted to go further before attaining the maturity to do so. Instead of quietly inhabiting and working with the newly developed structure for a time, the soul easily allows herself to be driven on and on. Are we not reminded of the scene in Paradise? The Creator God put Adam in the Garden of Eden and gave him all its splendor. He gave him many things to eat and spoke only one forbidding word: "But of the tree of the knowledge of Good and Evil thou shalt not eat, for in the day that thou eatest thereof thou shalt surely die."

But Man in Paradise would not wait until he had reached the stage at which he could eat of this tree and remain unharmed. It is Lucifer, the serpent, who drives the soul to expand beyond the limits in which she should remain according to the development of her capacities. She wants to know more than she is capable of knowing, and falls a prey to the powers of Earth and Death. It is like this for the growing child at puberty. Mary's Child is in possession of the divine wisdom hidden within her bodily nature. She should feel happy therein, but she is by no means content. Her immature soul, which wants to stretch further and further, urges her on. The desire to grasp everything before she is fully developed will seal her doom. At last, Mary's Child wants to open the thirteenth door as well. She has been warned that she must not open the door, for the time has not yet come. Her own heavenly being—in the form of the angels—warns her. But she is too much under the influence of temptation to listen to these voices. She has come into the mood of soul which precedes the fall into temptation.

Then she was silent, but the desire in her heart was not stilled, but gnawed there and pecked on it properly, and let her have no rest. And once when the angels had all gone out, she thought: "Now I am quite alone, and I could peep in. If I do, no one will know it." She sought out the key, and when she had got it in her hand, she put it also in the lock, and when she had put it in, she turned it round as well.

For Mary's Child this is a moment in which she is left to her own devices. The angels have withdrawn, and she is given up to her selfish wishes only. At such a moment the human being is left quite alone. Every wrong and criminal deed comes about in this way, when a human being suddenly feels himself deserted, and wants only to obey the gnawing urge in his heart.

The door flew open, and there she saw the Trinity sitting in fire and radiance.

In the fairy tale we find repeatedly mirrored those things which happen in the great cosmos and those which can be experienced by the human being himself. It is just this which gives the mysterious charm of the fairy story. At one moment it tells of the most sublime spiritual things, and at another of what is happening in the poor striving soul. In the heavenly sense the

Trinity means the harmonious interplay of the Father, the Son, and the Holy Spirit; and this is reflected in the three soul forces of thinking, feeling, and willing. When, at fourteen, the soul becomes more and more free, the time has come to begin the long struggle to bring harmony to its own forces which, to begin with, rage chaotically. It is inherent in the nature of evil that the erring way can lie in two directions. Mary's Child strays at first along the path that leads her too early to the great secrets of the spiritual world. The door which should not yet have been opened by her flies open, and reveals the Trinity, sitting in fire and radiance. So stands the young soul at the time of puberty, face to face with the great riddles of the world. Great beauty, wonderful light can sparkle at this age from the eyes and face of the growing child. In her deeds there often lives the fire of true enthusiasm. It sometimes reveals itself like lightning in thoughts which can touch even the essence of existence. A philosophy can arise which encompasses all the riddles of the world, and strives to solve them. On the other hand, a burning will seeks to be active. It would love to conquer the whole world, but must usually content itself with some comparatively meaningless occupation. For one child it may be a small discovery, for another the tailoring of a very special dress—and many content themselves in our days with some kind of often rather senseless achievement in sport. Feelings flood the heart. What today may be lovingly worshipped—a picture, a teacher, a friend—may tomorrow be violently thrown aside in hatred. The soul is full of ideals, but for the most part they are rather uncertain and vague. Superficiality and chaos become prevalent.

She stayed there awhile and looked at everything in amazement; then she touched the radiance with her finger, and her finger became quite golden.

Mary's Child had wanted to achieve the harmony of the three soul forces all at once, as quickly as possible. Now she suddenly finds herself overpowered by it all, and sees more than she can take in. She can not withdraw again, does not even want to, but only wants to share in the glory she does not yet deserve. So she touches the radiance with her finger—and a mark remains. One who had attained full maturity in life and was then face to face with the Trinity, would be able to receive what the spiritual world revealed. He would be able to feel the harmony in his being and the bright Sun Gold of Heaven would descend into his heart. There it would rest, hidden in his heart's ennobling forces. But Mary's Child, full of desires, can only touch the surface of what unveils itself before her. Nothing of the cosmic secrets can penetrate into her inner being. It is only on her inquisitive finger that something does remain. Although the fairy tale does not say, we can imagine that it is her forefinger. This sign of guilt on her finger is really a picture of the superficial and yet charming way in which the adolescent sets himself problems, solves them, and thrusts them aside again.

Immediately she felt a mighty fear. She banged the door violently and ran away. But, do what she might, her anguish would not quit her, and her heart beat continually, and would not become still. The gold, too, stayed on her finger, and would not go away, however much she washed and rubbed it.

We meet something which is beyond our understanding, and fear besets us. To stand worthily before a manifestation of the heavenly world fills us with fear. This fear is felt in the heart, because it is always in the heart that we first have a feeling of our destiny, and fear is almost always called forth by the guilt of unfaithfulness to our true destiny. The heart leaps with joy when the human being is able to take the right path in life, but it throbs with trembling fear when he has enmeshed himself in wrong-doing. Mary's Child now experiences the shudder of fear and notices that she cannot undo the wrong deed by simply washing the gold from her finger. It will not wash away. Just as little could Adam withdraw from his deed by hiding from his Father God.

It was not long before the Virgin Mary came back from her journey. She called Mary's Child to her, and asked to have the keys of heaven back. When the Child gave back the bunch, the Virgin looked into her eyes, and said: "You have not opened the thirteenth door, have you?"

"No" she replied. Then she laid her hand on the girl's heart, and felt how it beat and beat, and saw right well that she had disobeyed her orders, and had opened the door.

Mother Mary, who in the fairy tale represents the heavenly protection which still surrounded the child in the early period of life, knows the dangers to which the human soul is exposed when for the first time it is left to itself. Therefore, after a time of probation, she asks for the return of the heavenly keys. This indicates that the time has not yet come when she will allow the child to be free. The Heavenly Mother sees at once that the trial has not been surmounted. A great riddle seems to be hidden here. Each time, when at puberty the human being is reminded of the original sin of humanity, there can light up in the soul a hope that the state of Adam will be overcome. Usually this cannot happen, because the heart is not yet fully penetrated by the Divine Power which took upon itself the sin of humanity, and redeemed it. The meaning of the Heavenly Mother's journey and her return to the child might be expressed in the question: is the soul mature enough to be allowed to live on without fighting the great battles to which it must be exposed, if the original sin is still rampant within it? Mary recognizes that the little child she has taken into her care has not yet come so far. She has followed a selfish desire, and has touched the mystery externally. But a hope lies in the Mother of the Lord that even if the child has fallen to the one temptation—to draw wisdom to herself before she is worthy of it—she will at least be able to admit her wrong. Could she already hold to her true destiny? Perhaps she will not err in the other direction, and skid into callousness and lying. But Mary's Child has already lied for the first time—quickly, from a superficial and hasty thought, which so often happens at this age, when an answer is made up on the spot.

Mother Mary turns to the child's heart, but there within her heart is turmoil; it is cramped by the lie and fear leaves her no rest.

> Then she said once again: "Have you really not done it?"
>
> "No," said the girl for the second time.
>
> Then she caught sight of the finger that had become golden from touching the heavenly fire, and saw well that the child had sinned, and said a third time: "Have you not done it?"
>
> "No," said the girl the third time.

Three times the decisive question is put to Mary's Child, and we can feel how the soul becomes more and more enmeshed. The intellect succumbs quickly to the lie, and sullies the pure forces of thought. With torturing fear the lie wrests itself for the second time from the heart, this time soiling the innocence of feeling. And with the third question we must understand that now the child has to decide if the will too is to be seized by the lie. If this happens, fate must take a new turn and the soul will have to undergo sorrow after sorrow before it can be purified.

This threefold human sin is like a mirror picture of the threefold heavenly holiness of the Trinity seen by Mary's Child in fire and radiance. She had not been ready for such a sight and could not understand it, but she had in fact opened the door, although she had been forbidden to unlock it.

Before the third denial it seemed as though she could easily have been saved, had she been able to admit even to herself that she was in the wrong. Rigid defiance forced her to lie. She denied the destiny she herself had prepared. So she fell to the other side of the path of corruption and sealed her own fate for the immediate future.

Then said the Virgin Mary: "You have not obeyed me and besides that you have also lied; you are no longer worthy to be in Heaven."

The human soul is thrust to the Earth. Adam after the Fall is driven out upon the barren Earth to earn his bread by the sweat of his brow. Similar is the lot of the young person at the time of puberty. Ideals which a short time ago flashed through the soul have fled, and the hold of the earthly world gains in power. It is still the old sin of humanity in which the soul shares and from which it suffers.

Then Mary's Child fell into a deep sleep, and when she awoke, she lay on the Earth below, in the midst of a wilderness. She wanted to cry out, but she could bring forth no sound. She sprang up and wanted to run away, but whithersoever she turned, she was continually held back by thick hedges of thorns, through which she could not break. In the solitude in which she was enclosed, there stood an old hollow tree, and this had to be her dwelling place. Into this she crept when night came, and here she slept. Here too she found a protection from storm and rain.

Mary's Child has so far lost all connection with the heavenly world. She is quite alone, alone as only a human being can be through guilt. There is no escape. The forces of Earth have clutched her; hedges of thorns hold her fast. One might almost think, although the story does not relate it, that the child is held fast deep within that same forest, by which she had once lived. At that time misery had already reigned, when her destiny had still been connected with that of her parents. Now she has even lost her voice, and because of this she is entirely thrown upon her own resources, and is unable to call anyone to her aid. The sleeping in a hollow tree indicates how strongly she is surrounded by earthly forces. A hollow tree is the dead shell of a once living form, and this is the only shelter she can find.

But it was a miserable life, and bitterly did she weep, when she remembered how lovely it had been in heaven, and how the angels had played with her. Roots and wild berries were her only food, and for those she sought as far as she could go. In the autumn she picked up the fallen nuts and leaves, and carried them into the hole. The nuts were her food in winter, and when snow and ice came, she crept among the leaves like a poor little animal, that she might not freeze.

The soul deserted by the heavenly world, fed only on scanty fruits and roots of the dark Earth, feels miserable and forlorn, remembering the world from which it once descended. When the human soul is supported only by the dark powers of Earth and can evolve no further, it is in danger of losing its humanity and sinking to the level of the animal. The story expresses this very clearly. The girl has lost her voice and like an animal she cannot speak. It is even related that she has to hide "like a poor little animal."

Before long her clothes were all torn, and one bit of them after another fell off her. As soon as the sun shone warm again, she went out and sat in front of the tree, and her long hair covered her on all sides like a mantle.

More than ever Mary's Child is forced to adopt animal life. She loses all the protection that Mother Mary had given her. The clothes that fall from her body—and this we must not forget—were a gift from Heaven. We were told at the beginning that they were golden robes. Nothing of all this is left. Mary's Child has only her long hair to cover herself. The hair is a true symbol of the personal soul. Its lustre or its dullness, its silky softness or its wiry hardness is a vivid expression of the quality of the soul.

Thus she sat year after year, and felt the distress and the misery of the world.

It takes years indeed before the human being is able to surmount the crisis into which he may be driven during puberty. He finds support neither in himself nor in his physical surroundings. We should probably not be wrong in thinking that for Mary's Child it took until about the beginning of the twentieth year before she was released from the "distress and misery of the world." After this a new phase of development begins; the true individuality starts to work in the soul and seeks gradually to bring harmony into the chaos. The force which shone in upon the little child in the third year now begins to work powerfully in the adult human being. With this there comes about a dramatic change.

One day, when the trees were once more clothed in fresh green, the King of the country was hunting in the forest and followed a roe, and as it had fled into the thicket which shut in this part of the forest, he got off his horse, tore the bushes asunder, and cut himself a path with his sword.

The individuality must now learn to fully unite with soul and body. The soul has allowed herself to be seduced, has given up the heavenly world and has sunk to Earth. Here she feels imprisoned and delivered to loneliness and despair. The King and the royal Prince in the fairy tale always depict the spiritual being of man which must unite with soul and body. This happens as a struggle, with pain and striving. We see it so described in "Cinderella," in the "Goose Girl," in "The Handless Maiden" and in many others. In "Mary's Child," the description is given very clearly. The King must penetrate with all his might into the darkness and materiality of Earth in order to bring help to the fallen soul. He must push into the densest thicket; in other words, he must enter where matter is most concentrated and interwoven. As in the legends of Michael's fight with the Dragon, so here too the King must make a way for himself with his naked sword. Rudolf Steiner has shown how it is the lightening force of active thinking with which the Archangel Michael overcomes the passions arising from human instincts. The Dragon, flaring out of the fire of human craving and desire, threatens to befog the clarity of thought, and as long as the fire is not tamed, the soul is in danger of being thrown into darkness and chaos. The Archangel's sword of light brings quiet and peace.

The King is led in a special way—by a roe. The fairy story usually pictures the various powers of the soul in the form of animals. Turning for a moment to the story of "Little Brother and Little Sister," we find a good example illustrating the meaning of the roe. Grace and trust combined with a sanguine urge for movement form the picture portrayed by little brother, when he is transformed into a roe. He is uncontrolled, but there is no malice in him. At first he was to have become a tiger, and then a raging wolf, but he was saved from both transformations, and only at the third temptation does he fail to listen to the little sister's warning, and is turned into a roe. Passion and desire live in him, it is true, but everything is softened, and has something redeeming about it. In "Little Brother and Little Sister," it is the roe who helps the King to reach the maiden whom he will choose as his Queen. In "Mary's Child," it is also the roe, hunted by the King, which entices him into the thicket. With this touch the story delicately indicates the fact that the higher being is enabled to draw near by these forces of the soul that are still good in the human being. In this way the King discovers the beauty of the Child, in spite of all her misery. But what is it above all that he sees?

> When he had at last forced his way through, he saw a maiden of wondrous beauty sitting under the tree; and she sat there and was entirely covered with her golden hair down to the toes of her feet.

Despite the terrible environment and the poverty of her state he notices before anything else the golden hair streaming all around her, and this gold tells him of the true origin of the soul. She must have had her home in Heaven; that is why she is his, for the royal gold belongs to him.

> He stood still, and looked at her full of surprise; then he spoke to her and said: "Who are you? Why are you sitting here in solitude?" But Mary's Child did not answer, because she could not open her mouth.

The soul suffered deeply through her union with the darkness of Earth, but now the true individuality turns towards her, and offers the way to renewed ascent. But the maiden is still entangled by her guilt, and speech continues to be denied to her.

> The King continued: "Will you go with me to my castle?" Then she just nodded her head a little. The King took her in his arms, carried her to his horse, and rode home with her, and when he reached the royal castle, he caused her to be dressed in beautiful garments, and gave her all things in abundance. Although she could not speak, she was still so beautiful and charming that he began to love her with all his heart, and it was not long before he married her.

Let us recall the thread of the story. At first the soul is led into the Kingdom of Heaven in order to be prepared in beauty and quietness for the descent to Earth. But she falls into sin by being hasty and impatient. That causes her to return to Earth more quickly than she would otherwise have done. She also loses the faculty of speech, which was already developed at the age of three, at the time when Mother Mary came to fetch her. This faculty directs the way into the body. Speech belongs to the human spirit, but Mary's Child has lost her connection with it through her guilt, and has become dumb. The infant, already able to speak, was led into Heaven by Mother Mary for protection, and now the maiden is led by the King into an earthly castle. She is also given clothes again, and though it is not said that they were golden clothes, we are probably right in thinking that they are not to be compared with the heavenly clothes given her by Mother Mary.

> After a year or so had passed, the Queen brought a son into the world.

The King has become united with Mary's Child, but the soul still faces a long period of development. Again she has to undergo three trials, just as before she was questioned three times by the Heavenly Mother.

> Thereupon the Virgin Mary appeared to her in the night, when she lay in her bed alone, and said: "If you will tell the truth, and confess that you did unlock the forbidden door, I will open your mouth, and give you back your speech, but if you persevere in your sin, and deny obstinately, I will take your newborn child away with me."

The harmony of soul can only be attained during the course of life if the spiritual forces of the human being interpenetrate thinking, feeling, and willing. This interpenetration takes place gradually. It begins at the commencement of the twenties and should be completed in the middle of the thirties. A great problem is set for us through the Fall, whereby we enter the Earth realm prematurely. We can redeem the sin, if our egos are able to make good the evil our souls have committed. Every human being during puberty must to some extent come into contact with the sickness originating from the primeval fall into sin, but till the middle of his life he may receive the health for which he, as an individual, must strive. The human must however reconcile himself to the fact that he cannot stand aside from the original sin of humanity, however much he may refuse to admit that he himself shares in it. We were all present, as it were, when Adam fell. All this lives in Mary's Child quite unconsciously, of course, as in most human beings. When, as a sign of the union of the King with the Queen, the first child is born, the Virgin approaches the young Queen. Will she now be able to say "Yes" to her destiny, and consciously admit her connection with the guilt of humanity? She is sternly warned that if she still remains stubborn, she will lose her little son.

Then the Queen was permitted to answer, but she remained stubborn, and said: "No, I did not open the forbidden door." And the Virgin Mary took the newborn child from her arms, and vanished with it.

The Queen has not come far enough. She will still have nothing to do with the ancient guilt. The sign that for the moment her speech is given back might have been an indication to her what she ought to do, but she fails, and hardens her heart. With this she loses the first real result of her marriage, which no doubt should have been the spiritualizing of thought. The story does not give a definite picture for this, but we may he sure that this scene and the two following ones are really repetitions of the events that took place before the child was sent down to Earth. Then she lied three times to he Virgin Mary. Now something similar happens, but on another level. This time the soul should be able to decide freely; however, she is unable to do so, and severs herself from her true destiny.

Next morning, when the child was not to be found, there was a murmur among the people that the Queen was a man-eater, and had put her own child to death. She heard all this, and could say nothing to the contrary, but the King would not believe it, because he loved her so much.

It now happens to the Queen, as happens usually to a human being who is unfaithful to her own destiny, that the outer world begins to push her back, and tries to gain power over her. The surrounding world becomes merciless and unjust. This, however, is only a result of the fact that the individual being cannot stand firm. So there springs up a rumor that the Queen has destroyed her own child. Dreadful as this may sound, from the spiritual point of view it has an element of truth. The King in his great love allows nothing of the unfriendly agitation to touch him, and he remains true to the Queen, the soul belonging to him.

When a year had gone by, the Queen again bore a son, and in the night the Virgin Mary again came to her, and said: "If you will confess that you opened the forbidden door, I will give you your child back and untie your tongue; but if you continue in sin and deny it, I will take away with me this new child also."

Then the Queen again said: "No, I did not open the forbidden door," and the Virgin Mary took the child out of her arms, and went away with her to Heaven.

Even the great devotion of the King does not help Mary's Child to overcome the next trial. She refuses to recognize the guilt by which she is bound to the destiny of humanity, and so she loses her second child, who represents one of the three soul forces which should have been spiritualized.

Next morning, when this child also had disappeared, the people declared quite loudly that the Queen had devoured it, and the King's councillors demanded that she should be brought to justice.

It strikes to the heart of the people that the Queen has lost her second child too. Bad feeling grows against her, and unjust accusations are loudly expressed. Anger is kindled, and there is a call for retribution.

The King, however, loved her so dearly that he would not believe it, and commanded the councillors under pain of death not to say any more about it.

The power of the King is still supreme, because his love does not falter; he suppresses the outcry of the people with regal power.

The following year the Queen gave birth to a beautiful little daughter; for the third time the Virgin Mary appeared to her in the night, and said: "Follow me."

At the third trial can be seen what is really at stake from the way in which the Virgin appears and speaks to her child.

She took the Queen by the hand, and led her to Heaven, and showed her there her two eldest children, who smiled at her, and were playing with the ball of the world.

The two children who have been taken from the Queen are playing with the ball of the world. This is of special significance. It is not uncommon to see in old paintings—for example, in Dürer—the Jesus Child depicted as playing with the globe. The soul forces which remain withdrawn from Mary's Child because she will not acknowledge her guilt must be penetrated by the spirit. Ultimately they must be quickened by the redeeming

Spirit of Christ. This is indicated in the picture of the children who, like the Jesus Child, play with the ball of the world.

When the Queen rejoiced thereat, the Virgin Mary said: "Is your heart not yet softened? If you will own that you opened the forbidden door, I will give you back your two little sons."

The attention of Mary's Child is next drawn to what will happen if she does not admit her fault. She should admit her part in the original sin of humanity. The Holy Mother now stands before the Queen reminding her to do it.

But for the third time the Queen answered: "No, I did not open the forbidden door." Then the Virgin Mary let her sink down to earth once more, and took from her likewise her third child.

With the third denial of her deed, the Queen loses everything. She has given her destiny such a turn that she isolates herself from other men. She has forfeited the ascent to Heaven, and must leave behind her children. Once more she is thrust back into the depths of misery and is made to suffer.

Next morning, when the matter became publicly known, all the people cried loudly: "The Queen is a man-eater! She must be judged," and the King was no longer able to restrain his councillors. Thereupon a trial was held, and as she could not answer and defend herself, she was condemned to be burnt at the stake.

Even the King, the image of the true eternal Ego, can no longer save her, for she has poisoned all the three soul forces with her lies, and must dissolve the ties which bind her to the King. It is a subtle point in the story that she is guilty in her own inner life, but as far as the world is concerned, she is innocent, for she has not, in fact, devoured the children. Here the story shows a profound secret of human nature.

The wood was got together, and when she was fast bound to the stake, and the fire began to burn round about her, the hard ice of pride melted; her heart was moved by repentence, and she thought: "If I could but confess before my death that I opened the door."

Only now, when all at once she becomes fully conscious that she is being given over to death, is she ready to admit everything. She confesses her own destiny, and with this comes to see that she cannot disassociate herself from the destiny of mankind. At the sight of the wood that has been collected, and feeling the heat of the flames which threaten to consume her, the soul awakens at last to her own task. What once was taken upon Himself in full consciousness by the Savior that the sin of man might be redeemed, must again in due course be undertaken by each single human being. If only the individual can grow strong enough in himself openly to recognize his state, he will be able to receive the help of Heaven through Mary, the mother of the purified soul.

Then her voice came back to her and she cried out loudly: "Yes, Mary, I did it," and straightaway rain fell from Heaven, and extinguished the flames of fire, and a light broke forth above her, and the Virgin Mary descended with the two little sons by her side, and the newborn daughter in her arms.

The Queen repents, and the spirit descends upon her. The flames of destruction are cooled by the rain. The powers of soul that have been renewed in the heavenly world—thinking, feeling, and willing now penetrated by the spirit—are given back.

She spoke kindly to her and said: "He who repents his sin and acknowledges it is forgiven." Then she gave her the three children, untied her tongue, and granted her happiness for her whole life.

Speech, the Word, that power which is essentially human, is given back to Mary's Child. The soul has trodden an important path of development. She has at last attained her own higher self, and become united with it. The story shows this in that no further mention is made of the King. He has become one with Mary's Child and she regains happiness "for her whole life."

Briar Rose

INTRODUCTION

IT may be asked: what is the point of commenting again and again on these fairy tales of the Brothers Grimm? The answer is that the further this century advances, the greater grows the danger that the sources from which the spirit flows will become blocked. The children of today are the builders of the world culture of tomorrow. And if the children are not educated in the spirit for which they long, their hearts will become cold, and their brains will have become dry by the time they are old enough to shape this world for the people on earth. Nearly all Grimm's stories can act like a seed in the child's mind, which all unconsciously will grow and develop according to the deep meaning of the tale. Unfortunately, this possibility is killed by the silly pantomimes and movies to which thousands of children are taken year after year. In these performances the true content of the fairy tale is lost. Usually the writers enjoy showing how stupid the fairy tale is and allow themselves to spoil with their silly jokes the beauty of a story like "Cinderella" or "Snow White" or many others. The most popular stories especially are misused in this way. And the fact is that just these popular tales have the very deepest meaning. "Sleeping Beauty" or "Briar Rose"—*Dornröschen* ("Little Rose in the Thorns") as it is called in German—is one of these very popular stories and has many hidden riddles. It happens sometimes that we forget the charm of a landscape which we see every day, and in the same way we are so familiar with the story of Briar Rose that we may forget to ask what ideas are behind the tale. Therefore I am very grateful that I was obliged to live once again with the content of this fairy tale. A religion teacher in one of the Rudolf Steiner Schools told me that she had chosen Briar Rose for a lesson with very young children. It made a great impression on both her and the children, because they could all feel that a whole world was revealed in its wonderful pictures. And so I tried to find out if the teacher was right. After a time I became convinced that she was, and the children too.

It might be mentioned—although in the commentaries of other fairy tales it has already been said—that the children should be given nothing but the story. They need no explanation. The adult, however, should know what he or she is talking about and can become convinced in this way that he or she is helping the children for their future life by telling them these fairy tales.

Briar Rose

(Sleeping Beauty)

A LONG time ago there were a King and Queen who said every day: "Oh if only we had a child!" but they never got one.

But it happened once that the Queen was sitting in a bath, when a frog crept out of the water onto the land and said to her: "Your wish will be fulfilled; before a year has gone by, you will bear a daughter." What the frog had said, happened, and the Queen had a girl who was so pretty that the King could not contain himself for joy, and ordered a great feast. He invited not only his relatives, friends, and acquaintances but also the wise women in order that they might be kind and well disposed towards the child. There were thirteen of them in his kingdom; but as he had only twelve golden plates from which they should eat, one of them had to stay at home.

The feast was celebrated with all splendor, and when it ended, the wise women bestowed their magic gifts upon the child; the one gave virtue, the other beauty, the third riches and so on, with everything that one can wish for in the world. When eleven of them had just made their promises, suddenly the thirteenth came in. She wished to revenge herself, not having been invited, and without greeting anybody or even looking at anyone, she cried with a loud voice: "The King's daughter shall in her fifteenth year prick herself with a spindle and fall dead." And without saying a further word she turned round and left the room.

All were frightened, but the twelfth, whose wish still remained unspoken, came forward and, as she could not undo the evil sentence but only soften it, she said: "It shall be no death but a deep sleep for a hundred years into which the Princess shall fall."

The King, who would fain keep his dear child from the misfortune, gave the order that every spindle in the whole kingdom should be burned. But the gifts of the wise women were all given to the maiden, for she was so beautiful, modest, friendly, and understanding that everyone who saw her was bound to love her.

It happened that on the very day when she was fifteen years old, the King and the Queen were not at home and the maiden was left in the palace quite alone. So she went around everywhere, looked into rooms and bedchambers just as she liked and at last came to an old tower. She climbed up the narrow winding staircase and reached a little door. A rusty key was in the lock, and when she turned it, the door sprang open and there in a little room sat an old woman with a spindle, busily spinning her flax. "Good day, little old mother," said the King's daughter, "what are you doing there?"

"I am spinning," said the old woman, and nodded her head.

"What sort of thing is that, that rattles round so merrily?" said the girl, and she took the spindle and wanted to spin too. But scarcely had she touched the spindle when the magic decree was fulfilled, and she pricked her finger with it.

In the very moment when she felt the prick, she fell down upon the bed that stood there and lay in a deep sleep. And this sleep extended over the whole palace: the King and Queen who had just come home, and had entered the big hall, began to fall asleep, and the whole of the court with them.

The horses too slept in the stable, the dogs in the yard, the pigeons upon the roof, the flies on the wall; even the fire that was flickering in the hearth became quiet and fell asleep; and the joint left off sizzling, and the cook who was just going to pull the hair of the scullery boy, because he had forgotten something, let him go and slept. And the wind fell, and on the trees before the castle not a leaf moved any more.

But round about the castle there began to grow a hedge of thorns which every year became higher and higher till at last it surrounded the whole castle and grew beyond it so that there was nothing of it to be seen, not even the flag upon the roof.

But the story of the beautiful sleeping Briar Rose—for so the Princess was named—went about the country, so that from time to time Kings' sons came and wanted to get through the hedge into the castle. But they found it impossible, for the thorns held fast together, as if they had hands. The youths were caught in them, could not get themselves loose again, and died a miserable death.

After long years a King's son came again to that country and heard an old man talking about the thorn hedge; a castle was said to stand behind it in which a wonderfully beautiful princess, named Briar Rose, had been asleep already for a hundred years, and the King and the Queen and the whole court were asleep likewise. He knew too from his grandfather that many Kings' sons had already come and had tried to get through the thorny hedge but they had remained stuck fast in it and had died a sad death.

Then the youth said: "I am not afraid. I will go on and see the beautiful Briar Rose." The good old man might dissuade him as he would; he did not listen to his words. Now the hundred years had just passed, and the day had come when Briar Rose was to awaken again. When the King's son approached the thorn-hedge, it was nothing but large and beautiful flowers, which parted from each other of their own accord, and let him pass unhurt, and then again they closed behind him like a hedge. In the castle yard he saw the horses and spotted hounds lying asleep; on the roof sat the pigeons with their little heads under their wings. And when he entered the house, the flies were asleep upon the walls, the cook in the kitchen was still holding out his hand as if he would seize the boy and the maid was sitting by the black hen which she was going to pluck. So he went on further and in the hall he saw the whole of the court lying asleep and up by the throne lay the King and the Queen. Then he went on still farther and all was so quiet that a breath could be heard and at last he came to the tower and opened the door into the little room where Briar Rose was asleep. There she lay and was so beautiful that he could not turn his eyes away, and he bent down and gave her a kiss. But as soon as he had touched her with the kiss, Briar Rose opened her eyes, awoke and looked at him in quite a friendly way. So they went down together, and the King awoke and the Queen and the whole court and looked at each other with wide-opened eyes. And the horses in the courtyard stood up and shook themselves; the hounds jumped up and wagged their tails; the pigeons upon the roof pulled out their heads from under their wings, looked round and flew into the field; the fire in the kitchen rose up and flickered and cooked the food; the joint began to sizzle again; and the cook gave the boy such a box on the ear that he screamed; and the maid finished plucking the fowl.

And then the marriage of the King's son with Briar Rose was celebrated with all splendor and they lived merrily to the end of their days.

Briar Rose

COMMENTARY

A LONG time ago there were a King and a Queen who said every day: "Oh if only we had a child!" but they never got one.

This introduction points out in the simplest way that we are being led into an age in which changes take place. In olden times people usually had their children without thinking much about it—in a dreamy way. When these conditions came to an end, it was the sign of a new step in human development. This can already be seen in the Bible. It took Abraham a hundred years before his wife Sarah was allowed to have the son they wished for. And with Abraham a new age begins.

In fairy tales we frequently find that a child is anxiously expected, but difficulties arise in bringing the child down to earth. It hesitates, perhaps, to be exposed to the hindrances of the world. Remember "Rapunzel," "Daumesdick," "Die Nelke" and in a certain way "Snow White." Great contrasts are shown in these tales, as they occur also in real life. In some stories we see how in the mother, the father, or in both, lives the longing to have a child. This often means, in the language of the fairy tale, the longing for the coming of a new age. In other tales a situation is pictured absolutely opposite to the one described above. The parents already have their children but do not know how to manage, for they lack the means to feed them. Here people are so much entangled in the needs of life on earth that they can recognize only much later, after a long development, the blessing of a higher destiny in the children who are apparently so easily given to them. Thus it is in "Die drei Schlangenblatter," "Hansel und Gretel," "Der Gevatter Tod," or "Der Gevatter."

But it happened once that the Queen was sitting in a bath when a frog crept out of the water onto the land and said to her: "Your wish will be fulfilled; before a year has gone by, you will bear a daughter."

What the frog had said, happened, and the Queen had a girl who was so pretty that the King could not contain himself for joy and ordered a great feast.

The way in which the child is here announced to the mother is quite remarkable. It is not the Angel Gabriel as in the Bible; neither is it another unnamed Angel as in "Die Nelke"; nor is it meant to be only a symbolic picture as in "Snow White." It is the frog who makes the prophecy. He is the representative of the watery element just where it starts to border on the earthly. He is himself an inhabitant of both elements, the earth and the water. In his young days he still breathes through gills; in later life through lungs. He likes to live in the warm mud and so he is connected with the fertility of the soil. For mud prepares in the best way the growing life on the Earth. The fertilizing forces descending from the realm of the Moon find a specially suitable substance in mud. The mud of the river Nile has been known for thousands of years as the dispenser of life for the people living in Egypt. In medieval times, it was even commonly believed that life originated from mud. In that belief there still lived something of the old knowledge that into the damp element of muddy earth the fertilizing forces of the Moon could easily penetrate. The gods of fertility, too, were related to the region of the Moon. We may remember that the Greek Artemis became for the Romans Diana on Earth, and in Heaven, Luna, which is also the Latin name for the Moon. Gabriel, the Angel of the Annunciation, belongs also to the Moon.

Although in fairy tales the old wisdom is gradually vanishing, the higher knowledge shines through in a wonderful way. It is is also the case here, where the frog has to announce the birth of the child. He is the one who does it because he belongs—even though as a minor servant—to the realm of the Archangel Gabriel, who was allowed to announce to Mother Mary the coming of the Highest Being.

He invited not only his relatives, friends and acquaintances but also the wise women, in order that they might be kind and well disposed towards the child. There were thirteen of them in his kingdom; but as he had only twelve golden plates from which they should eat, one of them had to stay at home.

All the powers of the world are needed to bring man the right help for his development on Earth, according to his destiny. The highest forces have to be called upon for his protection and blessing. The Zodiac through which the Sun makes his way is twelvefold. We can see in old pictures of the human organism that a particular part of the body is connected to each sign of the Zodiac. The organ of the larynx is connected to the forces of the Bull; the region of the heart to those of the Lion. These cosmic forces shaping the human being are united by the Sun, which moves through the hours of the world's clock. The cosmic clock can also be imagined as a big table laid with plates. There would have to be twelve plates, and on each plate that food is served which a specific part of the human being needs for its growth. This table must be prepared by the Sun for the good of man's essential being and health. The plates could only be made from that material which belongs to the Sun, that is, from gold.

The righteous King in fairy tales is usually the servant of the good forces connected with light and brightness. When he wants to invite these heavenly powers for the full protection of his newborn child, he naturally has just twelve golden plates. This points to the twelve forces of the universe, united by the Sun. They have to bring man down to Earth in accordance with the Spirit of the Sun. But there are opposing powers who once rebelled against the realm of the Sun. For such a power no golden plate can exist any more. Although the King knows this, he is not awake enough to foresee the consequences of neglecting the adversary.

The feast was celebrated with all splendor, and when it ended, the wise women bestowed their magic gifts upon the child: the one gave virtue, the other beauty, the third riches and so on, with everything that one can wish for in the world.

It seems as if the King and his people felt quite satisfied with the idea of not inviting the one wise woman for whom no golden plate was available. This was thoughtless and dreamy. It belonged to a time which should come to an end, according to the fairy tale.

Evil has its influence and the effect on a person is worse if it is not opposed in full consciousness. This is soon shown in the story. Evil has to be encountered in evolution, and humanity is not allowed to overlook it. We must frankly oppose it; otherwise we will succumb all too easily.

When eleven of them had just made their promises, suddenly the thirteenth came in. She wished to revenge herself for not having been invited, and without greeting anybody or even looking at anyone, she cried with loud voice: "The King's daughter shall in her fifteenth year prick herself with a spindle and fall down dead." And without saying a further word she turned round and left the room.

The way in which a child comes to earth is connected with the Fall of Man. Everybody has the task of redeeming the Fall—a task which should not be forgotten. But the King of the tale did not want to acknowledge evil as a necessity of human evolution. Thus he calls evil to the great festival without knowing it. The thirteenth wise woman appears just at the moment when she is not expected and consequently can become most effective.

The problem arises: which power is it that works in such a disastrous way? With the help of Rudolf Steiner's teaching we can gradually gain an almost complete explanation of the events in the fairy tale. The powers of darkness are those divine beings who forsook the spirits of light. This separation is connected with the stars belonging to the sign of the Scorpion. Once this region in the sky was called the Eagle. At that time the forces emanating from it generated life and light. Later the powers of darkness spread their influence and those stars connected with them got the name of Scorpion. They are hostile to the Sun. The old Eagle was one of the four main star groups of the Zodiac: Bull, Lion, Eagle, and Man. In the course of time the two latter have changed their names.

From a certain time on, forces emanate from the Scorpion which are opposed to the Sun and are full of darkness. They harden the earth. According to Rudolf Steiner, the killing of life during the old Sun evolution was called "the sting of the Scorpion."* (So far as the evolution of the Earth is concerned, the influence of the Scorpion causes the development of Materialism in philosophy). The relationship of the Scorpion to the shape of the body is shown in the old illustrations. According to them, the Scorpion forms by its forces the human sex organs. Some paintings and old works of sculpture portray the sex organs as pierced by the sting of a Scorpion. It is usually a bull which is depicted in this way.

* Rudolf Steiner: *The Spiritual Hierarchies*, Dusseldorf, 1909
Rudolf Steiner: *Egyptian Myths and Mysteries*

The sexual organs developed for the first time when the Sun was standing in the sign of the Scorpion.* If we consider all this together, it becomes obvious that the twelve invited wise women are the messengers of the cosmos who guide human incarnation in a positive way. The thirteenth belongs to the evil powers who tempt people and lead them strongly into the hardening forces of the earth. At the time of puberty we are most exposed to these influences, thus, in great danger of falling prey to them. At this time desires start to play an important part in the life of young people—we are stung by the scorpion. In this fairy tale, instead of the sting we find the spindle, by which the princess will be pricked. She will then fall prey to death, caused by the evil forces. When will this happen? When she is fifteen years old—just at the time of adolescence. But though the evil powers may plot their deeds very cunningly, at some point they just miscalculate. This may happen through over-intellectualizing, or hurrying too much. It happens also in "Briar Rose." The evil fairy appears without any warning. The moment seems so dreadful because apparently no one is able to check her. She makes one great mistake, however. It is especially characteristic of these devilish beings that they can never wait long enough. Nothing could have saved the beautiful child if the thirteenth had come after the blessing of all the twelve wise women. But the evil fairy slips in after the eleventh, utters her curse of death and disappears. Her great mistake was that she came before the twelfth wise woman.

> All were frightened; but the twelfth, whose wish still remained unspoken, came forward and as she could not undo the evil sentence but only soften it, she said: "It shall be no death but a deep sleep of a hundred years into which the Princess shall fall."

Who is the twelfth? For what divine power does she stand? She can only represent the force which can redeem the Fall of Man. But Christ alone can lead Adam, who has been expelled from Paradise by his guilt, back into the spiritual realm. The appearance of Christ is connected with the sign of the Fishes. This is the reason why the Fishes are seen so often as a symbol of Christianity. In the catacombs they are found again and again on the altars and above the tombs. In the Zodiac, Pisces is considered to be the last sign, the twelfth, among the stars. Thus

* Rudolf Steiner Series No. XXXIII.

it becomes clear why the twelfth wise woman is the most powerful. She stands for the Christ, who has overcome death. She succeeds in doing the same for the beautiful child. But the old sin cannot be undone. Each individual must redeem it by his or her own destiny. Only then can a human being become worthy of mercy.

The Fishes are also the symbol of feet and hands. This is an accurate picture. In olden times it was known that the forces streaming from those stars were connected with the shaping of hands and feet. They are the organs which have the most to do with destiny and its fulfillment. We walk with our feet where destiny leads us, and we work with our hands in the world in such a way as our karma allows. We hear from Rudolf Steiner that Christ was once called the Master of Karma. Thus we can see from many sides that the Fishes are really Christ's symbol, but it can be called, as well, the sign of human destiny.

The King does not value the power of the thirteenth wise woman in the right way. Consequently he risks falling into the power of the dark forces. The Christ can save him, although his guilt cannot be redeemed without suffering. Thus not an eternal death but only a temporary one—the sleep of a hundred years—is prophesied as redemption for the neglect of evil.

The King, who would fain keep his dear child from the misfortune, gave the order that every spindle in the whole kingdom should be burnt. But the gifts of the wise women were all given to the maiden, for she was so beautiful, modest, friendly and understanding that everyone who saw her was bound to love her.

The King has shown by overlooking the might of the thirteenth wise woman, that he lacks the real wisdom a King should possess. By his following command he reveals how little he understands the true working of destiny, for it can easily be understood that his mistake will not be corrected by the simple order to destroy all the spindles in the empire. That idea was the product of shallow thinking. Both the command and the disregard of the evil fairy demonstrate the weakness of the King and the necessity for a new beginning, but this will become possible only by atonement of the guilt incurred through his weakness.

It happened that on the very day when she was fifteen years old, the King and the Queen were not at home and the maiden was left in the palace quite alone.

Time passes and the princess grows up. The time arrives when, in accordance with her stage of development, she has to unite herself deeply with the forces of the Earth. At this moment the child liberates herself from the influence of her surroundings. Their protection is taken away from her, and she looks suddenly with changed eyes—namely, with her own individual eyes—upon the world. The love which previously enveloped the child loses its might and she is left alone with herself. Thus the story relates that the Princess is left alone by her parents on the day when she becomes mature. Father and mother have lost their importance from now on.

So she went round everywhere, looked into rooms and bedchambers just as she liked and at last came to an old tower. She climbed up the narrow winding staircase and reached a little door. A rusty key was in the lock and when she turned it, the door sprang open and there in a little room sat an old woman with a spindle, busily spinning her flax.

A child left alone at that stage of life wants to explore everything thoroughly. Did not "Mary's Child," in the fairy tale of that name, do just the same when she was left to herself in her fourteenth year, while Mother Mary went away? The description in the fairy tale is very similar to a picture in a dream. Everyone who has spent time examining his or her dreams will remember that it is only necessary to find the right explanation for the picture to have it make sense. Experience with dream images shows that waking up can be depicted in many ways. The human soul visualizes itself coming back into the body. This usually happens so quickly that we have no time to remember the picture. Sometimes, however, it can be retained. We may observe that certain events turn up again and again in similar images without any external influence on the dreamer. The return of the soul into the body in awakening is often experienced as climbing up or sliding down a winding staircase. During sleep the soul is expanded widely, and must compress itself more and more when waking up, in order to adjust itself to the body. From outside, our bodies appear small and frail. How could that be better symbolized than by a little room into which we are obliged to enter through a small door with a rusty key? There is a deep meaning indicated by the fairy tale in the fact that this picture occurs just here. At the time of adolescence the child is developing in such a way that the soul becomes to a certain extent free. From now on the girl should not be so much ruled by her body, but should learn to use it as an instrument for the forces of her soul. With the advent of adolescence it depends solely on the individual whether he or she learns to act independently of the body, or remains ruled by it. In the terms used earlier it could be said: now it can be seen whether a person follows the laws of the Eagle or the Scorpion.

The mention of the winding staircase points to a decisive moment in the Princess' life. We are not only dependent on our own personal destinies but also on the destiny of the whole of humanity. It is obvious that in the maiden it is not a question of her own individual guilt. It is a critical moment of evolution through which everybody has to live during adolescence. The tempter is watching for his opportunity.

> "Good day, you little old mother," said the King's daughter; "what are you doing there?"
>
> "I am spinning," said the old woman, and nodded her head.
>
> "What sort of thing is that, that rattles round so merrily?" said the girl, took the spindle and wanted to spin too. But scarcely had she touched the spindle when the magic decree was fulfilled, and she pricked her finger with it.

If we try to find out who this tempter really is, who appears in the figure of the old woman, it suddenly becomes clear that it can only be the evil thirteenth fairy, who will know exactly when her time of vengeance has arrived.

It is remarkable how in any realistic scene of temptation, curiosity acts in a disastrous way. In the description of the Arch-temptation in Paradise, curiosity is already living in Eve. In "Mary's Child," curiosity is also an important element. Its consequences stick like a bad mark on her finger, stained with gold. In this story even the King's daughter, who is so beautifully represented in her innocence, is suddenly filled with a certain curiosity. She sees something which because of her father's order she has never been able to see before. Why curiosity wakes up in the soul at important moments can easily be understood. It holds good for the story of Paradise as well as for "Mary's Child," and many other legends and fairy tales—including, of course, Briar Rose—that the evil tempter tries to entice his victim into a stronger union with the earthly world than the lawful spiritual beings allow. Thus the way into matter, the way of research, is also led by a kind of curiosity.

Intellectuality is linked together with instinct and will to form a dangerous unity. Curiosity, too, "stings" us like the sting of the Scorpion, who injures the heavenly man to bring him down to Earth. Accordingly it is not so strange that the Princess exclaims out of curiosity: "What sort of thing is it that, that rattles around so merrily?" Her curiosity appears at the time of her maturity. She is taken hold of by the evil of mankind and is pricked by the spindle, the sting of the scorpion. As this takes place, she succumbs to the curse.

In the very moment when she felt the prick, she fell down upon the bed that stood there, and lay in a deep sleep. And this sleep extended over the whole palace: the King and Queen who had just come home, and had entered the big hall, began to fall asleep, and the whole of the court with them.

The spell has its effect, but in the form to which the twelfth fairy has transmuted it. Here is a secret which is deeply hidden in the story. What would have happened if the thirteenth fairy had been victorious? The girl would have died after the sting. That would have effected a total severing of her heavenly connection. She would have fallen a prey to the dark powers, like Adam after the Fall. But Christ gave back to Adam the life in the spirit by redeeming the deed of the first human. To find his way to this redemption, Adam had followed the law of destiny. Although he died—as the devil wanted him to do—yet he was also allowed to be resurrected. This was only possible when his guilt was wiped out. Those thoughts, and more, are touched on in the tale. The wicked fairy pronounced the spell over the beautiful child, and the twelfth fairy transmuted it for her. But further events show that the destiny of a single human being—in this case the King's daughter—is intimately connected with the fate of her whole surroundings.

Unable to oppose the power of evil, the King has thus exposed his child to the curse of death. This curse can only be alleviated by the mercy of the twelfth wise woman, the really Christian one. And now, in consequence of the King's failure, not only is the life of his child lost for the time being, but also he himself, the Queen, the whole court and even more, as will be seen, are involved in the future resurrection of the Princess.

The horses too slept in the stable, the dogs in the yard, the pigeons upon the roof, the flies on the wall; even the fire that was flickering in the hearth became quiet and fell asleep; and the joint left off sizzling, and the cook who was just going to pull the hair of the scullery boy, because he had forgotten something, let him go and slept. And the wind fell, and on the trees before the castle not a leaf moved any more.

The King's mistake involves not only human beings, but the whole of nature; animals, trees, even the wind are affected by the destiny which is the outcome of his guilt. In fairy tales events are shown to have larger implications than are usually supposed by present day people. The life of the individual is much more connected with the whole world than is usually supposed. What will happen on earth in the future really depends on us. If the right moment has been missed, it will be necessary to wait until the favorable time recurs, and destiny can be fulfilled.

Only the idea of reincarnation can bring sense into our lives. Through this alone, guilt and redemption reveal their true importance. We are led into earth existence in such a way that tasks are given to us which we have to fulfill. This holds good in small as well as in important things, and happens for each individuality according to his or her character and personality. If man remains deaf the first time to the call which sounds for him, he will have to hear it one day with greater intensity. It may then be painful for him. But if he remains deaf to the last, then his mistakes will be shown to him very clearly after death. And then he prepares himself, in the time after death, to do in a coming life what he neglected before. All this is the hidden wisdom in this fairy tale. The King is not aware of the necessities of his age. He does not realize that his task is to fight openly and in full consciousness against evil. So he drags all who live with him into misery. Although his child's future destiny can be foreseen, it cannot be fulfilled because of his own weakness. But without the hand of mercy, the future would mean death. In the life described by the story, he has missed his task. Thus he and all who belong to him have to undergo death, but a kind of death which leads again to life. That is the reason why this death is called in the story "a long sleep only." In this way we can understand the hundred years sleep which is mentioned. Everyone has to wait because the King has failed in his mission.

But round about the castle there began to grow a hedge of thorns which every year became higher and higher till at last it surrounded the whole castle and grew beyond it so that there was nothing of it to be seen, not even the flag upon the roof.

The death on earth from which we are allowed to wake up again after we have finished one life, means for us a time of inner consideration and preparation. Then externally, on the earth, our existence and our deeds may be forgotten. And over what we have done "the grass grows," as it is sometimes expressed. The fairy tale is even more exact; for over all the King has done, a thorny shrub grows, and what is behind the hedge must remain segregated and untouched by the earth's history. The right moment has to be awaited.

But the story of the beautiful sleeping Briar Rose—for so the Princess was named—went about the country, so that from time to time King's sons came and wanted to get through the hedge into the castle.

The idea of a mysterious and transformed future which lies ahead has remained as legend in the country. That this is so is shown by the fact that only the maiden is spoken of in stories and not the King. The spiritual reality remains, but hidden from the eyes of living men. If we want to speak in the language of the fairy tale, we have to say: on this side of the hedge of thorns is the world of our senses; beyond is the realm of the supersensible, unapproachable at present. Into that invisible region the King and all his empire were forced to withdraw. Destiny must be compensated through this deathlike sleep. When the right time has come, the connection with the earthly world will be rediscovered in its right form. Courageous people, princes, try repeatedly to penetrate to the other side. It is extremely interesting that only at this point in the story is the beautiful child, with whose growing up all these dramatic events are connected, called by her name: "Briar Rose" (*Dornröschen*, little rose in the the thorns). This name, not mentioned before, should be taken as an accurate depiction. The little rose blossoming behind the solid hedge of thorns can be imagined as a little red flame, which greets one gloriously, like a promise, behind the rigid thicket of the earthly world. We might be reminded of an even more powerful picture in the Bible: Moses hearing his call from the burning thornbush. What else is this thornbush but the image of the world of hardened earth into which the Pharoah thrusts his prisoners? Yet beyond the thicket burns the fire of the spirit. And out of the flame calls the voice of the Lord to Moses.

What is described in the Bible with the might and power of an event of elemental force is transformed in the fairy tale into tender beauty. This change is quite justified, for the red rose has become the symbol of the true love which Christ brought in its purity to this planet. When a person is blessed and baptized with the fire of the spirit, the pure rose of love can blossom in his heart.

The sleeping Briar Rose is a picture of the sleeping soul which, once awakened, brings to mankind the love awaited after the overcoming of evil.

The name of Briar Rose is a remarkable one. It is understandable that it is pronounced now for the first time, when the spiritual battle starts, and the princes stake their lives for the maiden.

> But they found it impossible, for the thorns held fast together, as if they had hands, and the youths were caught in them, could not get themselves loose again, and died a miserable death.

But the resistance is still too great. There is no lack of princes, that is, people who long for communication with the heavenly world. But the time in which they live is still too much ruled by the hardening and earthly forces. The way to the new world, transformed by the spirit, is still blocked by the hardening forces in the earth, symbolized by the thorny hedge. The dark powers are still strong, and kill those who fight for the spiritual world. We may remember that terrible moment when a much mightier Being than these young princes was crowned with thorns and had to endure the mocking of those men who could not look through the curtain of dark clouds which covered the sky.

> After long years a King's son came again to that country and heard an old man talking about the thorn hedge; a castle was said to stand behind it in which a wonderfully beautiful princess, named Briar Rose, had been asleep already for a hundred years, and the King and the Queen and the whole court were asleep likewise. He knew too from his grandfather that many Kings' sons had tried to get through the thorny hedge but they had remained stuck fast in it and had died a sad death.

A long time has passed. New conditions now exist, but the stories of the hidden castle are still told. And then something happens which often occurs when someone gifted with the forces of youth is ready to take on a new task to which he feels called. The old generation that wants to maintain the traditions of the past tries to avoid the work created by the new task.

The Prince, who feels that he must penetrate the thicket of the material world, gets a warning from an old man. Although the old man has experienced nothing himself, he remembers the frightening story once related to him by his grandfather.

Then the youth said: "I am not afraid, I will go on and see the beautiful Briar Rose." The good old man might dissuade him as he would; he did not listen to his words.

Inspired by the image of the beautiful maiden, however, the Prince can not be kept back. In this image we see the characteristic attitude of the old compared with the attitude of a new generation. The old generation believes that everything has to be continued as before. The old can become rigid in their conceptions and spread fear among those who have faith in evolution. The old man's intention may be the best in the world, but his soul is full of fear and he does not believe that circumstances can be changed.

Now the hundred years had just passed, and the day had come when Briar Rose was to awake again.

But this Prince is a special person. The other fighters were only the impatient precursors. They were not well guided. The Prince who now ventures out has the inner certainty that he must proceed now and just now! No old man, unable to distinguish between him and the others of whom the legend tells, can hinder this Prince.

When the King's son approached the thorn-hedge, it was nothing but large and beautiful flowers, which parted from each other of their own accord, and let him pass unhurt, and then again they closed behind him like a hedge.

The Prince arrives at the hedge just in time. He has felt, and recognized through his inner activity that he is ready and that the time is ripe too. He does not become paralyzed in his will by fear. He possesses the right attitude for a work of decisive importance. Thus he is able to penetrate the deadly thorns of a hindering and hostile world. And because it is the right moment, he sees also what lies in reality beyond these thorns. Our eyes are opened when we pierce through the world of senses. Then the eternal world of life expands in front of us and receives us. In this moment the cruel hedge of thorns is transformed. They become beautiful flowers belonging to the realm of life. The first step into the supersensible world is taken.

In the castle yard he saw the horses and spotted hounds lying asleep; on the roof sat the pigeons with their little heads under their wings. And when he entered the house, the flies were asleep upon the wall, the cook in the kitchen was still holding out his hand as if he would seize the boy and the maid was sitting by the black hen which she was going to pluck.

The Prince continues on, and the second step which he has to take to penetrate beyond the earthly world is shown to him. He comes to the region where the animals have their origin and where the soul in part belongs. Here he meets horses and dogs, flies, and a few human beings who symbolize lower stages of inner development in comparison with the people of the court. To make this clear, it must be remembered that in olden times the social order was quite different from today. Kings and people of the court had to possess a higher inner development than servants and working people. Here is the cook, who in a fit of rage is about to beat the scullery boy, and the kitchen maid whose capacity is not yet equal to more than plucking a hen.

So he went on further and in the hall he saw the whole of the court lying asleep and up by the throne lay the King and the Queen.

At the third step the Prince is led fully into the realm of humanity. There he finds the court, the King and the Queen. He passes them all and lets them sleep quietly. They do not seem important to him. He feels no connection with them and nothing further happens.

Then he went on still farther and all was so quiet that a breath could be heard and at last he came to the tower and opened the door into the little room where Briar Rose was sleeping.

At last, the moment arises when the Princess is to be awakened and led back into the physical world. Like Briar Rose, the Prince too has climbed up the small winding staircase. He will have to go back down to earth in the next moment. But he is not unconscious and he brings something home from his stay in the heavenly world. He has entered this world with the clear intention of accomplishing his task, and he has the new forces to do it.

There she lay and was so beautiful that he could not turn his eyes away and he bent down and gave her a kiss. But as soon as he had touched her with the kiss, Briar Rose opened her eyes, awoke and looked at him in quite a friendly way.

He now unites his strong being, his individuality, with the awakening soul. Because this is done at exactly the right time, the end of the hundred years, Briar Rose is allowed to wake up at once and begin a new destiny. For this she is ready with all her heart, and so she looks with friendly eyes on the Prince.

So they went down together and the King awoke and the Queen and the whole court, and looked at each other with wide-opened eyes.

Next it is told how Briar Rose, led by the Prince, walks back down the same stairway he has taken to find her. Everywhere the young couple appears, human beings are the first to awaken. Their past destiny is now resolved and the old spell is removed.

And the horses in the courtyard stood up and shook themselves; the hounds jumped up and wagged their tails; the pigeons upon the roof pulled out their heads from under their wings, looked around and flew into the field; the fire in the kitchen rose up and flickered and cooked the food; the joint began to sizzle again and the cook gave the boy such a box on the ear that he screamed; and the maid finished plucking the fowl.

The whole animal world wakes up also. In the castle the busy life can start again. What was interrupted before can be continued. In a humorous way it is pointed out in the kitchen scene that in the course of destiny nothing is lost. The scullery boy who has escaped in his previous life the pulling of his hair because of the important events in the palace, now gets a box on the ear when he wakes up again. The maid, too, has to resume her duties which have been interrupted, and continues to pluck the black hen. Nobody is spared his troubles.

And then the marriage of the King's son with Briar Rose was celebrated with all splendor and they lived merrily to the end of their days.

A new beginning becomes possible again. The first King was not able to protect Briar Rose, but the young Prince and future King is her lawful protector and can be united with the beautiful being. He could wake her up because he was led by his inner striving at the right time. And we can foresee that with guilt. His strong individuality, penetrated by freedom and consciousness, is able to unite itself with the soul who was beautifully matured for love. Now we understand why the old King was filled with such joy when his child arrived. He foresaw the new age; but a long development had to come before the fulfillment became possible.

The young couple fulfilled the task of their destiny according to the world powers who once stood at the cradle of Briar Rose to bless her with all the treasures of heaven. This moment reminds us of Adam's creation, when he was adorned also with celestial splendor. Because he failed, all people have still to suffer the effects of the Fall. Then there came the light of the Savior. The twelfth fairy, as His representative in the fairy tale, came to the aid of Briar Rose. The redemption of the thirteenth fairy's evil deed was accomplished to the satisfaction of the twelve wise women. This is expressed by the simple words at the end of the fairy tale: "and they lived merrily to the end of their days."

Thus it is pointed out that the evil thirteenth fairy has lost her game and that the twelfth has remained the victor, together with her sisters. So also the devil has lost his game, although Adam was expelled from Paradise—for the first Man was redeemed finally by the Christ.

The Handless Maiden

INTRODUCTION

Motto: I believe that in a fairy tale I can best express my mood of soul . . . Everything is a fairy tale.
Novalis, *Fragments.*

Since the publication of "Snow-White," with accompanying explanations, I have received many requests to do the same with another fairy tale. I have decided to comply with this request for the following reasons. As was declared in the introduction to "Snow-White," real fairy tales are of very great significance for young children. But they have a particular influence when the storyteller himself can believe in their content. This is possible, for these tales handed down to us by the brothers Grimm are based on an inner reality. If only we can discover the treasure lying hidden in these stories, their content can be brought to the children with the full force of conviction. The children themselves have a great power of understanding for the pictures in which this content is clothed. The interpretations of the pictures are to help adults understand the hidden meaning which lives in the fairy tales, and are, of course, meant only for them and not for the children.

"The Handless Maiden"* has been chosen because it is among the most wonderful of the Grimm fairy tales, though it is far less popular than "Snow-White" and many others. It relates momentous events in the story of human development and sheds light on many riddles of life.

If this commentary results in the children hearing "The Handless Maiden" more often than hitherto, the aim of the work will be attained. It need only be added—and those acquainted with children will know this —that children are never tired of hearing the same story over and over again.

* The author is indebted to Miss Olive Whicher for her help in translation.

Great care has again been taken in the translation that the English should remain faithful, word for word, to the original text. Only then is justice really done to the fairy tale.

The Handless Maiden

A MILLER had fallen gradually into poverty, until he had nothing left but his mill and a large apple tree behind it. One day, when he had gone into the forest to fetch some wood, an old man whom he had never seen before approached him and said: "Why do you trouble yourself with chopping wood? I will make you rich if you will promise me what stands behind your mill."

The Miller thought, "What else could this be but my apple tree?" So he said "Yes" and agreed to give it to the stranger.

The other, however, laughed derisively and said: "After three years I will come and fetch what belongs to me." And then he went away.

As soon as the Miller reached home his wife came to him and said: "Tell me, Miller, whence comes this sudden flow of riches into our house? All at once every chest and cupboard is filled, and yet no man has brought anything in; I cannot tell how it has happened."

The Miller, in reply, told her: "It comes from a stranger whom I met in the forest, who promised me great treasures, and I agreed to give him in return what stands behind the mill: we can very well let him have the great apple tree."

"Ah, my husband!" exclaimed his wife, "That was the Devil; he did not mean the apple tree, but our daughter, who stood behind the mill sweeping the yard."

The Miller's daughter was a beautiful and pious maiden, and during all the three years lived in the fear of God without sin. When the time was up, and the day came when the Evil One was to fetch her, she washed herself quite clean and made a circle around herself with chalk. The Devil appeared quite early, but he could not approach her; so, in a rage, he said to the Miller: "Take away from her all water, that she may not be able to wash herself; else I have no power over her. " The Miller did so, for he was afraid. The next morning came the Devil again, but she had wept upon her hands so that they were quite clean.

Then again he could not approach her, and furiously said to the Miller: "Cut off both her hands, or else I cannot get at her."

The Miller was horrified, and said: "How could I cut off the hands of my own child?"

But the Evil One threatened him, saying: "If you do not, you are mine, and I will take you yourself away!" The father was frightened and promised to obey.

Then he went to the maiden and said: "My child, if I do not cut off both your hands, the Devil will fetch me, and in my fear I have promised it. Now help me in my trouble, and forgive me for the wickedness I am about to do to you."

She replied: "Dear father, do with me what you will; I am your child." Thereupon she laid down both her hands and had them cut off. The Devil came for the third time. But so long and so much had she wept on the stumps that they were clean nevertheless. So he had to withdraw and had lost all power over her.

The Miller now said to her: "I have received such great wealth through you that I will care for you most dearly all your life long."

But she answered: "Here I cannot remain; I will go away. Compassionate men will give me as much as I require."

Then she had her mutilated arms bound behind her back, and at sunrise departed on her journey, and walked the whole day long till night fell. Then she reached a royal garden and by the shimmer of the moon she saw trees standing there, bearing most beautiful fruits, but she could not enter, for there was water all round. Since, however, she had walked the whole day without tasting a morsel, she was tormented with hunger and thought: "Ah, would I were there, that I might eat of the fruit; else shall I languish with hunger." So she kneeled, implored God, and prayed. All at once there came an angel, who closed a sluice in the water, so that the ditch was dry for her to pass over. Then she went into the garden, and the angel with her. There she saw a tree with fruit, beautiful pears, but they were all numbered. She stepped up and ate one off the tree with her mouth to appease her hunger, but no more. The gardener watched her do it, but because the angel stood by her, was afraid and thought the maiden was a spirit; so he remained quiet and did not dare to call out or to talk to the spirit. As soon as she had eaten the pear she was satisfied, and went and hid herself in the bushes.

The next morning the King to whom the garden belonged came down, and counting the pears, found that one was missing. He asked the gardener whither it had gone, as it was not there and neither was it lying under the tree. The gardener replied: "Last night a spirit came, who had no hands, and ate one pear with her mouth."

The King then asked: "How did the spirit come over the water? And whither did it go after it had eaten the pear?"

The gardener answered: "One clothed in snow-white garments came down from heaven, closed the sluice and stopped the water, so that the spirit could walk through the ditch. And because it must have been an angel, I was afraid and neither called out nor questioned it. As soon as the spirit had eaten the pear, it went back again."

The King said: "If it be as you say, I will this night watch with you."

As soon as it was dark the King came into the garden, bringing with him a priest, who was to address the spirit, and all three sat down under the tree and watched. At midnight the maiden crept out from under the bushes, stepped towards the tree and again ate a pear from it with her mouth, while the angel clothed in white stood by her. Then the priest went towards her and said: "Art thou come from God or from Earth? Art thou a spirit or a human being?"

She replied: "I am no spirit but a poor human, deserted by all, save God alone."

The King said: "If you are forsaken by all the world, yet I will not forsake you." And he took her with him to his royal castle, and because she was so beautiful and pious, he loved her with all his heart, ordered silver hands to be made for her, and made her his bride.

After a year had passed by, the King was obliged to go to war, so he commended his mother to take care of the young Queen and said: "When she comes to child bed, sustain and care for her well, and send me a letter immediately." Soon afterwards the Queen bore a beautiful son, and the old mother wrote immediately and gave him the joyful news. The messenger, however, rested on his way by a brook, and being weary with his long journey, fell asleep. Then came the Devil, who had always tried to harm the pious Queen, and changed the letter for another, wherein it was said that the Queen had brought a changeling into the world. As soon as the King had read this letter, he was frightened and much troubled; nevertheless, he wrote an answer to his mother, that she should take great care of the Queen until his arrival. The messenger went back with this letter, but on his way rested at the same spot, and went to sleep. Then the Devil came a second time, and put another letter in his pocket, wherein it was said the Queen and her child should be killed. When the old mother received this letter, she was struck with horror, and could not believe it. So she wrote another letter to the King, but she received no other answer, for the Devil again placed a false letter in the messenger's pocket and in this last it said that she should preserve the tongue and eyes of the Queen as a token.

But the old mother wept that such innocent blood should be shed; so she caused a hind to be fetched by night, and cut out its tongue and eyes and kept them. Then she said to the Queen: "I cannot let you be killed, as the King commands; but you must remain here no longer. Go forth with your child into the wide world, and never return here again."

Thus saying she bound the child upon her back, and the poor wife went away with weeping eyes. Soon she entered a large wild forest, and there she fell upon her knees and prayed to God. The angel appeared and led her to a little cottage, and over the door was a shield inscribed with the words "Here may everyone live freely." Out of the house came a snow-white maiden, who said: "Welcome, Lady Queen!" and led her in. Then she took the little boy from the Queen's back and put him to her breast, so that he should drink, and laid him on a beautifully covered bed.

Then the poor woman asked: "How do you know that I am a queen?"

And the white maiden answered: "I am an angel sent from God to tend you and your child." In this cottage she lived seven years and was well cared for, and through God's mercy to her, on account of her piety, her hands which had been cut off grew again.

Meanwhile the King had come home again from the campaign, and his first thought was to see his wife and child. Then his mother began to weep and said: "You wicked man! Why did you write to me, that I should put to death two innocent souls!" And showing him the two letters which the Evil One had forged, she continued: "I have done as you commanded;" and she brought him the tokens—tongue and eyes. Then the King began to weep so bitterly for his dear wife and son that the old mother pitied him and said: "Be comforted, she lives yet! I caused a hind to be secretly slain, from which I took these tokens; but the child I bound on your wife's back. I bade them go forth into the wide world, and she promised never to return here, because you were so wrathful against her."

"So far as heaven is blue!" exclaimed the King, "I will go, and neither will I eat nor drink until I have found again my dear wife and child, if they have not perished of hunger by this time."

Thereupon the King set out, and for seven long years sought his wife in every stony cleft and rocky cave, but found her not; and he began to think she must have perished. And all this time he neither ate nor drank, but God sustained him.

At last he came into a great forest, and found there the little cottage whereon the shield was with the words, "Here may everyone live freely." Out of the house came the white maiden and she took him by the hand, and leading him in said: "Be welcomed, O King! Whence comest thou?"

He replied: "I have wandered about for nearly seven years, seeking my wife and her child; but I cannot find them."

Then the angel offered him meat and drink, but he refused both, and would only rest a little while. So he lay down to sleep, and covered his face with a napkin.

Now went the angel into the chamber where sat the Queen, with her son, whom she usually called "Sorrowful," and said to her: "Come with your child; your husband has arrived." So she went to where he lay and the napkin fell from his face.

The Queen said, "Sorrowful, pick up the napkin and cover again your father's face." The child picked it up and placed it over his face; and the King, who heard in his slumber what passed, gladly let the napkin fall again from his face.

At this the boy became impatient, and said: "Dear mother, how can I cover my father's face? I have no father on this earth. I have learned the prayer 'Our Father which art in Heaven,' and you have told me my father was in heaven—the good God. How should I know such a wild man? He is not my father."

As the King heard this, he raised himself up, and asked the Queen who she was. She replied: "I am your wife and this is your son, Sorrowful." But when he saw her living hands, he said, "My wife had silver hands." "The merciful God," said the Queen, "has caused my hands to grow again." And the angel, going into the chamber, brought out the silver hands and showed them to him.

Only now he was convinced that they were his dear wife and child, and he kissed them gladly, saying: "A heavy stone has dropped from my heart." Then the angel of God fed them both once more and they went home to his old mother.

There was great rejoicing everywhere, and the King and Queen celebrated their marriage once again and lived happily until their blessed end.

The Handless Maiden

COMMENTARY

A MILLER had fallen gradually into poverty, until he had nothing left but his mill and a large apple tree behind it.

In fairy tales an important part is usually played by a man's occupation. In the Miller we have a man who is closely related to the elemental world; he is connected with everything that is watery. The mill only works when the mill stream is full and flows properly. In olden times the water element signified not only the physical fluid, but also the life forces transmitted through water. The Greeks and the Romans knew of the water-beings, the undines, which dwelt in streams and rivers. Peoples of earlier evolutionary epochs were really gifted with the ability to see these creatures. In earlier times, human beings still lived deep in the mists of a dream world, and did not experience themselves as self-contained personalities. The outer world did not have for them the clearly defined contours which it has for us today. On the other hand, they experienced all the more intimately the world which lies hidden behind what is visible. Then came a transitional time in the course of human development. The supersensible world veiled itself more and more, and yet human beings were not mature enough to grasp the things of the Earth with the individuality of the ego. The Miller is such a being, no longer so able to penetrate the sphere of the water element as before. And for this reason he has fallen into poverty.

He has evidently no more real work for the mill, although it is one of the possessions which remains to him. The mill is like the human heart. Just as the latter is set in motion by the fluid, by the streaming blood, so the mill is driven by the flowing water of the mill stream.* That which lives in our blood we can understand with our heart; and as the heart beats rhythmically,

* Only in the time following Harvey does the idea appear in Physiology that the heart is a kind of pump. Author.

so too the mill clappers strike in rhythm. The dreaming speech of the heart is born of rhythm, and the heart still understands well the world of the elements. But the Miller has forgotten this speech, and that is why he has gradually become poor. Now temptation threatens him. This is shown in the beginning of the story by the image of the apple tree, which is still one of his possessions. This apple tree is the same symbol of temptation as that found in the biblical Paradise story.

The fairy tale begins, then, at a very dramatic moment. The Miller has arrived at a turning point in life. He has become poor, still has his mill, but has no more work for it because he has lost the speech of the heart—which unites him with the elements. Here, it is his other possession, the apple tree, which becomes significant for him. He is, as it were, ripe for temptation. This, moreover, is a favorite situation in which to begin a fairy tale. "Rumpelstilzchen" begins in almost the same way: "Once upon a time there was a Miller and he was poor . . . " and the tale arises out of a situation quite similar to that of the story with which we are now concerned.

> One day, when he had gone into the forest to fetch some wood, an old man whom he had never seen before approached him and said: "Why do you trouble yourself with chopping wood? I will make you rich if you will promise me what stands behind your mill."
>
> The Miller thought, "What else could this be but my apple tree?" So he said "Yes" and agreed to give it to the stranger.
>
> The other, however, laughed derisively and said: "After three years I will come and fetch what belongs to me." And then he went away.

In the temptation scene we see the misery of the Miller. He must fetch wood and chop it, instead of living from the profit of his mill. He has a lot of hard work to perform. Here the tempter meets him. This happens for the first time, for we are assured that he had never seen the old man before. As soon as the Miller is promised riches, he is so fascinated that he neither recognizes the tempter nor reaches further with his thoughts than to the mill and the apple tree. All else disappears from his memory.

> As soon as the Miller reached home his wife came to him and said: "Tell me, Miller, whence comes this sudden flow of riches into our house? All at once every chest and cupboard is filled, and yet no man has brought anything in; I cannot tell how it has happened."
>
> The Miller, in reply, told her: "It comes from a stranger whom I met in the forest, who promised me great treasures, and I agreed to give

him in return what stands behind the mill: we can very well let him have the great apple tree."

"Ah, my husband!" exclaimed his wife, "That was the Devil; he did not mean the apple tree, but our daughter, who stood behind the mill sweeping the yard."

At this point we hear from the wife—who is less infected with earth-sickness—that the newly acquired riches can only come from the Devil. What has the unhappy father promised? What stands behind the mill? The apple tree is indeed there—but it only points to the act of temptation, because the Miller no longer knows the speech of the heart. Had he not given in, he would have realized that something else might be standing behind the mill: his daughter. The daughter is the young, pure soul, the bearer of the future, which must unfold itself. She will have to conquer the earth with greater understanding than the old Miller. We see the failure of the father. It is not, indeed, that the new forces are missing altogether. They already live as a seed behind his heart—the mill—but in the moment of temptation he forgets them. This is of no great interest to the Devil, since it is above all the daughter whom he wants. He wants just these young soul forces, in order to undermine the future development of the new human being. In Faust, too, Mephistopheles says: "Most of all I love the full, fresh cheeks." In contrast to this youth and freshness, the Devil appears in the fairy tale as an old man, and immediately afterwards the delicacy and great purity of the daughter are described:

The Miller's daughter was a beautiful and pious maiden, and during all the three years lived in the fear of God without sin.

The past weighs upon her, the sin of her father, but she herself has kept all her purity in spite of the riches, which, as is to be seen from a later remark, the Miller fully enjoyed. It may be mentioned that in "Rumpelstilzchen," too, we hear of a miller "who was poor, but had a beautiful daughter."

When the time was up, and the day came when the Evil One was to fetch her, she washed herself quite clean and made a circle around herself with chalk. The Devil appeared quite early, but he could not approach her; so, in a rage, he said to the Miller: "Take away from her all water, that she may not be able to wash herself; else I have no power over her. "

Here we see that the Miller's daughter, too, has a connection with the water powers. She has quite a new relationship to them, however. They serve the renewal of her life in the sense that through them she attains the purity of her soul. Water is used in baptism; holy water is sprinkled before the entry into the church, and from various legends we learn how the Devil is always angry when he is sprinkled with this holy water. Sometimes it even drives him to flight, as incense does. The daughter has drawn a magic circle around herself with pure chalk, and washed herself with water, which possesses the forces of purity. So the Devil cannot come near her, and it is understandable when he becomes infuriated and vigorously demands that the Miller remove all water from her.

The Miller did so, for he was afraid. The next morning came the Devil again, but she had wept upon her hands so that they were quite clean. Then again he could not approach her . . .

It is indeed her purity that matters. For now, when water is taken away from her, she is able through her own power to make use of the water which streams out of her eyes in order to remain pure. Nothing in the fairy tale seems to be without significance, and we notice that it is her hands which she washes clean. In this image the story shows how we can win our way on Earth through struggle and action. But our actions are connected with our hands.

. . . and the Devil furiously said to the Miller: "Cut off both her hands, or else I cannot get at her." The Miller was horrified, and said: "How could I cut off the hands of my own child?" But the Evil One threatened him, saying: "If you do not, you are mine, and I will take you yourself away!" The father was frightened and promised to obey. Then he went to the maiden and said: "My child, if I do not cut off both your hands, the Devil will fetch me, and in my fear I have promised it. Now help me in my trouble, and forgive me for the wickedness I am about to do to you." She replied: "Dear father, do with me what you will; I am your child." Thereupon she laid down both her hands and had them cut off.

Now the father succumbs entirely to the temptation. But his daughter is still bound to him by blood, and the blood tie still works strongly in her. She has a pure soul, but is not yet independent as a personality. For this reason she does not struggle against her father, but allows everything to happen. "Do with me what you will; I am your child." The reader or listener will experience at this point a definite feeling that with the severing of her hands and consequent flowing of blood from her stumps, the maiden's severs her connection with her father.

The inner tie between them is broken.

The Devil came for the third time. But so long and so much had she wept on the stumps that they were clean nevertheless. So he had to withdraw and had lost all power over her.

Again we see the effects of the maiden's purity, which streams out of her from within. The powers of inner life, shown in her tears, wash all the blood away. She has now released herself from the blood tie with her father. In the cleansing of the stumps it is indicated that she has also begun to cleanse herself of the original sin of her father. We are reminded of the entirely contrasting picture of Lady Macbeth: "What! Will these hands n'er be clean?" Despite all the scrubbing of her hands, she is not cleansed of her sin, and in her thoughts she cannot escape from hell. "Hell is murky."

The Miller now said to her: "I have received such great wealth through you that I will care for you most dearly all your life long." But she answered: "Here I cannot remain; I will go away. Compassionate men will give me as much as I require."

Then she had her mutilated arms bound behind her back, and at sunrise departed on her journey, and walked the whole day long till night fell.

When the Devil has gone, the Miller wants to somehow make up for what he has done. But he cannot undo the deed—the great change in the maiden is inexorable. She can have nothing more to do with her father, and so can no longer stay at home. Should she stay, she would have to share in the riches and bounties given by the Devil, and this she will not do. She is able to leave because she no longer feels herself bound by family ties. She also has confidence in the goodness of the people whom she will find on her way. Unhappily, she cannot rely completely on herself, because she no longer has any hands. Yet she even allows her arms to be bound behind her back as a sign that this does not come into question at all. The extent to which she breaks with the past we can see from the fact that from this moment on, no further mention is made of the Miller in the whole fairy tale.

Then she reached a royal garden and by the shimmer of the moon she saw trees standing there, bearing most beautiful fruits, but she could not enter, for there was water all round. Since, however, she had walked the whole day without tasting a morsel, she was tormented with hunger and thought: "Ah, would I were there, that I might eat of the fruit; else shall I languish with hunger." So she kneeled, implored God, and prayed.

We can clearly see that the Miller's daughter must now begin her life anew. Before the severing of her hands, her ego had hardly been able to make an appearance. It was still entirely bound to the family. Now she must develop it herself, and seeks the means to do so. This, however, takes time. At first we see that in the material world alone she can come no further; she is exhausted and needs real help. In the distance is the realm of the King. As we have noted in other commentaries, in many fairy tales the King is the picture of the personal ego of the human being. This is quite evident, for example, in "Snow-White." In the distance she sees the royal garden, but she cannot yet simply go inside. Before she can do this, she must withdraw from ordinary life and enter once more the living world of dreams.

In this tale we see once again how water has a certain relationship to both worlds. On this side of the water is the trouble-filled world of earthly events, while on the other side is the life-giving world of the super-sensible. Until now it had seemed sufficient to the maiden to possess the power of the water, the purity of the life forces, in order to be victorious over the Devil. Now a further step is indicated in the story. She must cross over the water. It is not a question of her ability to remain in the material realm, nor of her desire to do so. She wishes to be on the other side of the water in order to reach the domain of the King. This she cannot do without help. We are even shown what kind of life forces these are. They are Moon forces. Water has indeed its secret connection with the Moon—we need only think of the ebb and flood of tides, of the influence exerted by the different phases of the Moon on rainfall, and so on. So the maiden without hands sees, across the water, in the light of the Moon, the flourishing garden. Here she quite consciously begs for higher help, which is given to her. In the parents' house it was the unconscious power of her inner purity which helped her; she only wept, or she simply washed herself, but she asked for nothing consciously. Now it is all different.

So she kneeled, implored God, and prayed. All at once there came an angel, who closed a sluice in the water, so that the ditch was dry for her to pass over. Then she went into the garden, and the angel with her. There she saw a tree with fruit, beautiful pears, but they were all numbered. She stepped up and ate one off the tree with her mouth to appease her hunger, but no more. The gardener watched her do it, but because the angel stood by her, was afraid and thought the maiden was a spirit; so he remained quiet and did not dare to call out or to talk to the spirit.

She receives the help for which she implores and is led into the realm where she can be sustained. This is the contrasting picture to that of the Temptation. She is led into a garden full of fruit, like the garden of Paradise, but here it is not of the apples which the soul eats. She takes a pear, and although she is exhausted and hungry, she contents herself with what she needs "but no more." With this it is clearly shown how different is the disposition of this striving soul from that of the father who fell into temptation.

The gardener watched her do it, but because the angel stood by her, was afraid and thought the maiden was a spirit; so he remained quiet and did not dare to call out or to talk to the spirit. As soon as she had eaten the pear she was satisfied, and went and hid herself in the bushes.

The episode with the gardener is inserted in order to show that the Miller's beautiful daughter is really not as yet in full possession of the individual ego. The gardener therefore cannot tell whether or not she is a living human being.

The next morning the King to whom the garden belonged came down, and counting the pears found that one was missing. He asked the gardener whither it had gone, as it was not there any more and neither was it lying under the tree. The gardener replied: "Last night a spirit came, who had no hands, and ate one pear with her mouth." The King then asked: "How did the spirit come over the water? And whither did it go after it had eaten the pear?"

The gardener answered: "One clothed in snow-white garments came down from heaven, closed the sluice and stopped the water, so that the spirit could walk through the ditch. And because it must have been an angel, I was afraid and neither called out nor questioned it. As soon as the spirit had eaten the pear, it went back again."

The King said: "If it be as you say, I will this night watch with you."

All is now prepared in a most dramatic way for the first meeting of the Miller's daughter with the King. This meeting of the developing soul with the individual ego must happen at first in the realm on the other side of the water—not yet in the earthly world, although everything is prepared for this also to take place. This is to be seen in that the King, as representative of the ego forces, displays a kind of thinking which is characteristic of the Earth. He counts, and as the result of counting the pears he knows that one is missing. He can reckon, and knows what subtraction is. There lives in him a clearly-defined intellectual power, which is necessary for the life of the human ego upon Earth. A further symptom of this is his behavior to the gardener. He does not find it enough only to listen to this account of what happened, but wants to see for himself if all of it is really true. "If it be as you say, I will this night watch with you."

As soon as it was dark the King came into the garden, bringing with him a priest, who was to address the spirit, and all three sat down under the tree and watched. At midnight the maiden crept out from under the bushes, stepped towards the tree and again ate a pear from it with her mouth, while the angel clothed in white stood by her. Then the priest went towards her and said: "Art thou come from God or from Earth? Art thou a spirit or a human being?" She replied: "I am no spirit but a poor human, deserted by all, save God alone."

The King said: "If you are forsaken by all the world, yet I will not forsake you." And he took her with him to his royal castle, and because she was so beautiful and pious, he loved her with all his heart, ordered silver hands to be made for her, and made her his bride.

After a year had passed by, the King was obliged to go to war, so he commended his mother to take care of the young Queen and said: "When she comes to child bed, sustain and care for her well, and send me a letter immediately." Soon afterwards the Queen bore a beautiful son, and the old mother wrote immediately and gave him the joyful news. The messenger, however, rested on his way by a brook, and being weary with his long journey, fell asleep. Then came the Devil, who had always tried to harm the pious Queen, and changed the letter for another, wherein it was said that the Queen had brought a changeling into the world. As soon as the King had read this letter, he was frightened and much troubled; nevertheless, he wrote an answer to his mother, that she should take great care of the Queen until his arrival. The messenger went back with this letter, but on his way rested at the same spot, and went to sleep. Then the Devil came a second time, and put another letter in his pocket, wherein it was said the Queen and her child should be killed. When the old mother received this letter, she was struck with horror, and could not believe it. So she wrote another letter to the King, but she received no other answer, for the Devil again placed a false letter in the messenger's pocket and in this last it said that she should preserve the tongue and eyes of the Queen as a token.

All goes well at the castle as long as the King is present; nothing is heard of the Devil and his attacks on the Queen. This is because the human being can always shield himself from evil as long as he lives consciously with his own ego. Then the Queen awaits a child. If we observe a pregnant woman, it is easy to see that she is with her own individual forces far less deeply in her body than normally. For this reason the form of the body becomes lost to a great extent, and usually the features of the face also change at this time. The woman becomes less her own self. She must really withdraw herself to some extent from her physical body, in order to give place to the other incarnating soul. This fact is shown in that the King must leave the Queen. The absence of the King on the one hand, and the birth of the child on the other, of course attract the Devil once more. He had not forgotten the Queen, but in the presence of the King he was powerless. Now, however, that the King has departed, he feels the urge to destroy both the striving soul of the Queen and also the child. We are shown here that the future is what most interests the Devil. He wants to hinder all development. And now he works as the real spirit of lies. He could lead the Miller astray simply with the promise of riches, but he comes nowhere near the King. He can work his devilry now only by approaching the messenger, who is not at all awake. The King remains free of all guilt. He has a wonderful helper in his mother, who becomes for the Queen the representative of the King. This is a very special touch in the fairy tale. The old mother is the picture of the old powers that are still good, and can appear immediately in a selfless way when the strong power of the ego is absent. This old mother is the exact opposite of the Miller. She embodies the good forces from the past, which can always remain full of blessing when they manifest themselves free from all self-seeking. The Miller represents the outworn forces that desire to maintain themselves egotistically, and therefore so easily fall a prey to the tempter. The old mother knows exactly what is right—the Miller knew it no longer—and so she takes the only right step possible.

But the old mother wept that such innocent blood should be shed; so she caused a hind to be fetched by night, and cut out its tongue and eyes and kept them. Then she said to the Queen: "I cannot let you be killed, as the King commands; but you must remain here no longer. Go forth with your child into the wide world, and never return here again."

Thus saying she bound the child upon her back, and the poor wife went away with weeping eyes.

Now the Queen must depart once more. We see that she is far more innocent in her flight from the Devil now than at the time when she was still the Miller's daughter. The curse, however, still weighs upon her and upon her child. The inherited sin passes from generation to generation. This is shown in a strange repetition in the fairy tale. At first we recognized the human sin in the severed hands, and the arms she had bound to her back. At her second departure, where the importance is obviously attached by the Devil less to the Miller's daughter than to her son, this son is bound upon her back, before she goes away.

Soon she entered a large wild forest, and there she fell upon her knees and prayed to God. The angel appeared and led her to a little cottage, and over the door was a shield inscribed with the words "Here may everyone live freely."

Her departure indicates a withdrawal from the physical world for a certain time. Just as in "Snow-White," the image of the great forest points to her entrance into the world of the elements. Snow-White, too, found an unusual little house in the forest, the house of the seven dwarfs, the elemental spirits. "Here everyone may live freely," points also to this living world. Here in this world she will not suffer from want; everything she needs is to be had freely in the little house. Whenever "The Land of Plenty" is mentioned in a fairy tale, it indicates this world of life forces. There, a paradisal existence reigns, and life is "free."

Out of the house came a snow-white maiden, who said: "Welcome, Lady Queen!" and led her in. Then she took the little boy from the Queen's back and put him to her breast, so that he should drink, and laid him on a beautifully covered bed.

From all this we see that the Queen really sojourns in a world other than the physical world. The child at once receives nourishment and is cared for by a white being; it is really "freely" tended.

Then the poor woman asked: "How do you know that I am a queen?"

And the white maiden answered: "I am an angel sent from God to tend you and your child." In this cottage she lived seven years and was well cared for, and through God's mercy to her, on account of her piety, her hands which had been cut off grew again.

In this world of life, or of the etheric as Rudolf Steiner* has called it, the rhythm of seven plays a great part. Snow-White comes into the house of the seven dwarfs. In our own life this rhythm is a very important one. Think only that the physical matter of our bodies is almost completely renewed in about seven years; or that the crisis in certain forms of pneumonia takes place after seven days. Many other examples of this kind could be mentioned. It is therefore no wonder that the Queen spends seven years in this realm. It is of course also the land of healing, the region in which healing can take place. For this reason her hands are able to grow again, and she has no more need of the silver hands she received from the King. Now her real hands reappear, but for this, the gracious activity of the elemental world is necessary.

Meanwhile the King had come home again from the campaign, and his first thought was to see his wife and child. Then his mother began to weep and said: "You wicked man! Why did you write to me, that I should put to death two innocent souls!" And showing him the two letters which the Evil One had forged, she continued: "I have done as you commanded," and she brought him the tokens—tongue and eyes. Then the King began to weep so bitterly for his dear wife and son that the old mother pitied him and said: "Be comforted, she lives yet! I caused a hind to be secretly slain, from which I took these tokens; but the child I bound on your wife's back. I bade them go forth into the wide world, and she promised never to return here, because you were so wrathful against her."

"So far as heaven is blue!" exclaimed the King, "I will go, and neither will I eat nor drink until I have found again my dear wife and child, if they have not perished of hunger by this time."

The King returns. This means no less than that the individual ego, after its sojourn in the physical world, returns to see how it fares with the soul. But the Queen is no longer there. She has nearly fallen prey to the Devil. On learning this, the King rises up and resolves to go in search of the Queen. He knows too, where he must seek her. She is not to be found in the physical world. That is why he says he will seek her "as far as heaven is blue"—it is the elemental world of which he speaks. And he will not eat or drink—that, too, he could only do if he were not seeking her in the physical world.

* See Rudolf Steiner, *Occult Science* and many other works.

Thereupon the King set out, and for seven long years sought his wife in every stony cleft and rocky cave, but found her not; and he began to think she must have perished. And all this time he neither ate nor drank, but God sustained him.

At first, even so, he looks for her in the earthly world. The stony clefts and rocky caves are mentioned and a rocky cave always means emphasis on the earthly forces—according to some legends the earthly birthplace of Jesus was a rocky cave. But the Queen is not there. Only when he reaches the great forest does he at last draw near to the place he is seeking—the supersensible world, as has already been shown—and only there can the reunion take place.

At last he came into a great forest, and found there the little cottage whereon the shield was with the words, "Here may everyone live freely." Out of the house came the white maiden and she took him by the hand, and leading him in said: "Be welcomed, O King! Whence comest thou?"

He replied: "I have wandered about for nearly seven years, seeking my wife and her child; but I cannot find them."

Then the angel offered him meat and drink, but he refused both, and would only rest a little while. So he lay down to sleep, and covered his face with a napkin.

Now went the angel into the chamber where sat the Queen, with her son, whom she usually called "Sorrowful," and said to her: "Come with your child; your husband has arrived." So she went to where he lay and the napkin fell from his face.

The Queen said, "Sorrowful, pick up the napkin and cover again your father's face." The child picked it up and placed it over his face;

Now the whole story assumes more and more the quality of a dream, and we feel as we read that everything must now resolve itself. We may easily feel inclined to ask why the way has been so difficult, but this is now clearly shown. Before a person can truly achieve the union of the soul with the full individuality, he or she must usually go through painful experiences. We learn of this in many forms through the accounts of the ancient mystery initiations. In the fairy tale this fact is brought home to us when we are finally told the name of the child, for the first time. The Queen has called the child "Sorrowful."

And the King, who heard in his slumber what passed, gladly let the napkin fall again from his face. At this the boy became impatient, and said . . .

The King finds great joy in his slow awakening, and wishes to repeat the game with the child; but this child of the future, who will never more fall prey to the Devil, can bear the spinning of dreams no longer and wants to understand everything clearly.

"Dear mother, how can I cover my father's face? I have no father on this earth. I have learned the prayer 'Our Father which art in Heaven,' and you have told me my father was in heaven—the good God. How should I know such a wild man? He is not my father."

Now is revealed the essence of the situation. The Queen was unable to find the way directly to the fullness of her ego, because she always called to God and depended upon Him. In this way she unfolded her wonderful purity, but was not entirely ripe for the union with her human ego. She had not even told her child that he had an earthly father; she always had only the thought of the heavenly Father in her mind.

As the King heard this he raised himself up, and asked the Queen who she was. She replied: "I am your wife and this is your son, Sorrowful."

Now for the first time, in answer to the question of who she is, can she declare herself belonging to the King. Now she knows that she belongs to the ego, which has also gone through the pain of this world. She does not answer, as once before when asked the question: "I am no spirit, but a poor human, deserted by all save God alone." But she answers: "I am your wife, . . . " and the child, too, who belongs to the future, is his son, Sorrowful. To be able to live in the world as an individual, independent being requires the experience of great pain, which leads the individuality to ever higher development. The God who drove Adam out of Paradise promised him a life of sorrow and sweat.

But when he saw her living hands, he said, "My wife had silver hands." "The merciful God," said the Queen, "has caused my hands to grow again." And the angel, going into the chamber, brought out the silver hands and showed them to him.

Only now he was convinced that they were his dear wife and child; and he kissed them gladly, saying: "A heavy stone has dropped from my heart."

There is still to be felt a slight hesitation in the King's

behavior. The wife whom he had known had received silver hands from him, and now she stands before him with real hands. This must, of course, be so, for the silver hands still bore the memory of the old blood guilt of the Miller. Now this guilt has been cleansed through all the suffering of the King and Queen. Herein lay the blessing of God, who had accepted the sacrifice of the struggling human soul and human ego. This is why the Queen now has her natural hands once more. The King recognizes this, and a stone falls from his heart!

Then the angel of God fed them both once more and they went home to his old mother.